Death leaves a heartache no one can heal.

Love leaves a memory no one can steal.

Gentle Comforts

For Women Grieving the Loss of a Beloved Life Companion

KATHLEEN A. PARIS

GENTLE COMFORTS
For Women Grieving the Loss of a Beloved Life Companion
Kathleen A. Paris

Editing by Gregory F. Augustine Pierce
Cover and text design and typesetting by Andrea Reider
Copyright © 2024 by Kathleen A. Paris

Published by ACTA Publications, 7135 W. Keeney Street, Niles, IL 60714
www.actapublications.com 800-397-2282

ISBN: 978-0-87946-730-2
Library of Congress Number: 2024934250

Printed in the United States of America by Total Printing Systems
Year 30 29 28 27 26 25 24
Printing 10 9 8 7 6 5 4 3 2 First
Text printed on 30% post-consumer recycled paper

Contents

Contents

Contents

DEDICATION

To my husband,
Matt Cullen,
the best person I ever knew.

My Story

Dear sisters, I was happily married for twenty-five years to a very wonderful man. He was kind and thoughtful, smart, strong, funny, handsome, courageous, a loving father and husband. He could save you if you had a heart attack. (He was a paramedic.) He could fix your computer for you. (He was a business data analyst.) He could make you laugh. He could cook you the best Thanksgiving dinner you ever ate.

We were so happy together. A lot of the time, we didn't even need to use words to communicate. One of us would think something and the other would answer out loud.

Having Matt as my life partner gave me wings to do things I probably wouldn't have done without his encouragement, like publishing books and consulting around the world. Matt Cullen, my husband, died in 2018, taken by lung cancer. Losing him was the worst thing that ever happened to me.

So the reflections, journaling questions, and recipes here come from my own experience. I want to share with you what brought me comfort, what kept me going, and what I have learned about grieving. I hope this book will bring you comfort and hope as well.

Kathleen A. Paris
Madison, Wisconsin
Valentine's Day 2024

How to Use This Book of Gentle Comforts

*D*ear sisters, we are a sorority no one wants to be part of. We have all loved a partner who is no longer living. Yet here we are and I am glad that, at least, we can be together. My hope is that *Gentle Comforts* will be a support to you after the death of your mate, your companion, your husband, your spouse, your lover. Your grief is a natural and normal response to your loss, but we all can use encouragement and support as we move through it.

Look over the topics in the Contents pages and read those that fit the moment. Looking at the topics would be a great thing to do frequently, as our feelings and needs will change as time goes on. Yes, you could go straight through the book in order, perhaps doing one topic per week.

More likely, however, is that you will page through this book until you find something that speaks to what you are going through. Maybe you will want to read some of them more than once.

Each of the entries also includes journaling questions, inviting you to respond in writing. You can jot responses right in this book. If you prefer, you can write your thoughts in a separate journal book of your choosing. (I use spiral-bound notebooks.)

Journaling about how we feel and what is happening in our lives can be a real comfort.

Plus, with each topic you will find a simple, nutritious, delicious recipe that makes just two portions. I have made these dishes myself over the years and recently redesigned them to make smaller servings. (The recipe sources I am aware of are listed in the Recipe Index.) You can share one portion with a friend you invite over or take to her or his house, or one portion can be enjoyed immediately and the other the next day or frozen for a future time when you need that particular comfort food. You may even decide to double a favorite recipe when you feel like cooking for others.

Jot your own comments in the "Notes" section at the end of a recipe or in the back of the book. Keep track of ingredients you substituted or what you thought of the recipe.

Here's the thing. Even when we don't feel like making nutritious food for ourselves, it's essential that we do so for our physical and emotional energy in order to endure and move through our grief. We all deserve to be well-cared for, especially as we deal with the loss of our beloved.

If you want to read more from a particular author or research study I have mentioned, please see "References" in the back of the book.

I benefitted greatly from grief therapy. I encourage anyone going through what we are facing to also consider professional support, either through a mental health professional or grief group. We don't have to go it alone, but we do need gentle comforts to help us through.

Cooking for Yourself

We need and are worthy of healthy, home-cooked food without preservatives or mysterious chemicals. For those of us who are accustomed to cooking for at least two people (or if our mate did most of the cooking), it is an adjustment to cook for oneself, but so worthwhile! Not only can you maintain or improve your own health by cooking for yourself, but research shows that cooking can help with depression and grief.

I remember a dear auntie who was in her eighties stirring a boiling pot of pasta and saying, "If you don't cook for yourself, you don't eat!" The recipes in this book that I make at home for myself use fresh, unprocessed ingredients. (Not one canned soup recipe was allowed in!) Calorie counts are not included for the recipes, but most are naturally low in sugar and salt and use healthy oils. If you have suggestions for making any recipe better, please send feedback to info@actapublications.com.

I found that I needed a few different kitchen items in cooking just for me. You may also find these useful:

1. Instant-read food thermometer, particularly helpful for chicken.
2. Immersion or stick blender for blending of hot soup.
3. 10-ounce ramekin or smaller ones for the desserts.
4. Small baking dish (4 x 6 or 5 x 5).

5. "Spider." A wire spoon for fishing out vegetables or pasta or anything you are cooking in hot liquid. This handy utensil from Asia can prevent burns.
6. A food scale.
7. Bullet-type blender for smoothies.
8. Really Optional: Toaster oven and air-fryer to save energy costs.

Recipe Abbreviations

tsp.=teaspoon
T.=tablespoon
F.=Fahrenheit
oz.=ounce

Early Days

*D*ear sisters, our hearts are broken. We have lost the one we love. Our job at first is simply to survive.

Early on, when we have many duties to tend to around death, we need to ask for help from family, friends, neighbors, hospice professionals, our place of worship. We are in no shape to do it all.

Here are the most basic do's and don'ts for early days.

Please Do

- Do get outside once a day, if only to stand for a few minutes and breathe fresh air.
- Do take naps or rest in a dark, quiet place.
- Do drink liquids frequently to stay hydrated (alcoholic beverages don't count).
- Do drink smoothies and eat soup if it's too hard to eat anything else.
- Do let the tears come freely.
- Do ask for help.
- Do write feelings and thoughts on paper if it is comforting.

Please Don't

- Don't make any financial or housing decisions.
- Don't drive if feeling unsure about it.
- Don't feel you have to please other people
  while you are in such pain.

When we lose someone, it feels like we must be the only person who has suffered this much pain. We are isolated in our own bubble of misery. Yet since people have been on Earth, we have lost people we love dearly. It is part of being human.

Our grief is in direct proportion to the love we experienced. So we look at each other with sorrow-filled eyes and say, " I am so sorry for your loss. I've been where you are. We will lean on one another."

- What are the things you most cherish and appreciate about the one you have lost?

Yogurt Smoothie

Refreshing, filling, easy to make, easy to eat.

Ingredients	Directions
1 6-oz. container of yogurt (any style or flavor you like) Handful of fresh or frozen fruit (about ½ cup) ¼ cup of orange juice or any real fruit juice. 2 or 3 ice cubes	Place all in the blender or bullet-blender and blend till ice cubes are liquified.

Notes

Remembering

*D*ear sisters, we may be in a state of shock for a long time. When the day comes around that is the day of the week or month we lost our mate, we will probably re-live the day over and over. That is normal. We must let ourselves do that and let ourselves feel how we feel.

Every day, try to add in some activities that are comforting or at least distracting—a walk outside, a warm bubble bath or shower, a coffee break with a neighbor, a call or text to a friend, a movie, a nap, a swim, a visit to the zoo, a game of golf—whatever gives a mental and spiritual break from reliving the loss.

It can be helpful to write down some things we *want to remember* from the past weeks and months. Possibly we were surprised by someone's thoughtfulness or extra effort or compassion. Or was there an especially beautiful moment in the midst of the pain? Writing about these things is for ourselves. Downloading onto paper captures moments that touched our heart. Writing may help clear some space in your mind.

- What are some experiences and thoughts from the past weeks or months you want to remember?
- What would you want to share with your beloved?

....

....

....

....

....

....

....

....

....

....

....

....

Comforting Noodles

Ingredients	Directions
1½ cups egg noodles, un-cooked 2 T. Parmesan cheese, shredded 1 T. butter 1 T. olive oil ½ tsp. dried basil (or 1 tsp. fresh basil, chopped) ⅛ tsp. dried thyme 1 garlic clove, crushed ¼ tsp. salt **Garnish** Chopped fresh parsley	1. Cook noodles according to package directions, omitting any extra salt or oil. 2. Add remaining ingredients and toss to coat. 3. Remove garlic clove before serving.

Notes

The Dreaded Mail

Dear sisters, we might dread the mail. Those white envelopes flood our mailboxes—insurance, notifications, requests for information, forms to fill out, unwanted advertisements. It is overwhelming. Sometimes even cards and letters of condolence can be too much to open.

If you feel you cannot face all the mail, here is a suggestion. Get two baskets or two boxes and put cards and personal letters in one and bills and business envelopes in another. Open them when you can in the next week or two. We just cannot ignore the mail or let it migrate to various parts of the house.

We will surely want to send thank you notes to people who sent flowers or gifts or memorials or who were a special support. This can seem like an undoable challenge. Opening mail and writing thank you notes are the perfect tasks for which to ask for help.

For the business correspondence, someone you trust—a son or daughter or close friend—can help you sort out the bills and urgent communication from things that can wait. Many of those things can actually wait a few weeks even though they all feel terribly urgent. This will help prioritize our energy.

Some of the form letters might not even make much sense, so do ask for help. Having assistance can ensure the bills are paid on time and late fees avoided. This same trusted person or persons can also check email for us until we are up to doing that.

Even if someone sits with us and puts addresses and stamps on the thank-you notes, it can help us move through it. My sister did this for me and it made all the difference. Just having her sitting at the table with me was a comfort.

Think about the kinds of mail,
and the amount of mail,
showing up in your mailbox.

- What mail is most urgent to tend to?
- Do you need to ask for help?
- Who could help you?

Elegant Chicken

It's elegant because it's easy!

Ingredients	Instructions
1 boneless, skinless chicken breast (6-8 oz.) Mayonnaise to cover chicken (about 1/4 cup) 1/4 cup grated Parmesan cheese (to cover) ½ tsp. or more of your favorite seasoning blend (seasoned salt, Italian seasoning, *herbes de Provence,* lemon pepper, etc.)	1. Preheat oven to 350° F. 2. Place on a baking sheet and spread mayo over the chicken breast. 3. Sprinkle with Parmesan and seasoning blend. 4. Bake for 25-30 minutes depending on size of the breast and oven accuracy. A meat thermometer should reach 165° F.

Notes
- For easier cleanup, bake on parchment paper on the cookie sheet

Journaling

Keeping a journal helps you create order
when your world feels like it's in chaos.
You get to know yourself by revealing
your most private fears, thoughts, and feelings.

University of Rochester Health Center

Dear sisters, for me, journaling was a wonderful tool. It offered a chance to shut out the noise and be present to my own thoughts. In writing every day, I discovered things I hadn't even known about myself.

This journal is just for us. It will not judge us or blame us for feeling the way we do. We can pour our hearts out and drip tears on the pages. It's all good. The mere act of labeling a feeling (sadness, anger, loneliness, fear, etc.) can take some of the heat out of it. Labeling a thought or feeling—putting words to an emotion—causes changes in our brains that can help us deal with it, according to UCLA Professor Annette Stanton in a recent *Wall Street Journal* article.

Another real plus of journaling is that we can look back later and see how far we have come. We recognize things that were difficult early on we can now do easily.

Even if we don't consider ourselves to be great writers, it's OK! We have important thoughts to get out and things to say. Don't worry about spelling or grammar or complete sentences. Sometimes just a list of words or phrases will be plenty. (We can even draw stick figures or emojis.)

- If I wrote a note today to my beloved, I would say…
- I wish…
- What I need right now is…

Blueberry Cobbler

Enjoy the fresh burst of blueberries—
sweet, but not too sweet.

Ingredients	Directions
5 T. white sugar, divided 3 T. flour 1 T. uncooked rolled oats 1 T. light brown sugar 1 T. walnuts, chopped ½ tsp. lemon zest 1 tsp. lemon juice ½ tsp. vanilla extract, divided ¼ tsp. salt ⅛ tsp. cinnamon 2 T. butter 2 cups blueberries 1 T. cornstarch 1 tsp. brandy (optional)	1. Place two 6-oz. ramekins on a baking sheet lined with parchment paper. A small loaf pan will work fine too. 2. In a medium mixing bowl, combine 3 T. of white sugar, flour, oats, brown sugar, walnuts, lemon zest, 1/4 tsp. of vanilla extract, and the cinnamon. 3. With a pastry blender or clean hands, work the butter into the flour mixture until crumbly. 4. Chill the crumble mixture in the freezer for 30 minutes.

5. Preheat oven to 350° F.
6. In a large bowl, combine the remaining 2 T. of white sugar with the salt, lemon juice, and the last ¼ tsp. of vanilla extract.
7. Stir in the blueberries, cornstarch, and brandy (if using).
8. Divide the berry mixture between the ramekins and top each with the crumble mixture.
9. Bake until browned and the berries are bubbling, 35-40 minutes.

Notes

- The blueberries should not be soaking wet. I dry them on a dishtowel.
- The parchment paper is to make cleanup easier, as the ramekins will be quite full.

Sleep

When we are tired,

we are attacked by ideas we conquered long ago.

Nietzche

*D*ear sisters, many, many people working through grief have sleep problems. This can be trouble falling asleep or staying asleep or waking up every day at 4:00 a.m., or all of these—even if you slept like a log in the past.

I turned night into day when I first lost my husband. I thought nothing of cooking or exercising at 2:00 in the morning. I seldom knew what time it was. When I finally got into bed, the empty space beside me and his pillow brought on sobs until I was so stuffed up I had to get up anyway.

Grieving is exhausting, and yet sleep often eludes us. Experts recommend a regular bedtime routine without screen time. Some other tips include:

- Keeping your bedroom dark and cool.
- Turning off phone notifications.
- Avoiding screen time altogether in the evening.
- Keeping daytime naps short (30 minutes or less).

When having trouble getting to sleep, give it thirty minutes. Then get out of bed and do something non-electronic and non-alcoholic.

Try deep breathing. (Breathe in for 4 counts through your nose, hold it for 4, and exhale for 6 counts through your mouth. Repeat at least 10 times.) This can be calming to body and mind.

- Read a book or magazine.
- Meditate or pray.
- Have some hot chamomile or other herbal tea.
- Make a piece of toast.
- Listen to soothing music.
- Listen to on-line sleep sounds (white noise, rain, cats purring, etc.)
- Listen to a recorded book (my sleep aid of choice).
- Listen to an uplifting podcast.
- Look outside at the stars.
- Take a warm bath.
- Write about how you are feeling.
- Add calming essential oils to a diffuser (lavender, chamomile, vetiver, etc.).
- Try falling asleep in a recliner or on the sofa.
- Sleep on your love's pillow and/or side of the bed.
- Cuddle up in a body pillow or pregnancy pillow to feel snug.

When we are consistently sleep-deprived to the point of feeling ill or desperate, it's time for professional medical help. Similarly, if the challenge is sleeping too much and barely being able to get out of bed, this is also the time to get professional help. Seeking medical or psychological support shows our strength and determination.

- How have you been sleeping?
- What seems to work the best for you in getting to sleep? For staying asleep?
- What other sleep strategies do you want to try?

EZ Baked Fish Fillets

The fish steams in the oven and tastes so fresh and light.

Ingredients	Directions
Fillet of cod or sea bass (about 8 oz.), thawed 1 green onion, white and tender green parts, sliced ¼ tsp. salt Pinch of black pepper 2 tsp. minced parsley 3 lemon slices 1 T. plus 1 tsp. water (sauce ingredients on next page)	1. Preheat oven to 350°. 2. Arrange fish in small baking dish and sprinkle with green onion, salt, pepper, and parsley. 3. Top with lemon slices and pour water around the fillet. 4. Cover with a loose tent of foil and bake for 25-30 minutes until flaky. Cod is done at 145°F. 5. For sauce, combine all ingredients and chill for 30 minutes.

2 T. sour cream

1 T. plain yogurt

1 T. green onion (white and green parts), finely sliced

1 tsp. lemon peel, grated fine

Pinch of fresh dill

Pinch of white pepper

⅓ cup cucumber, peeled and chopped fine or grated

Notes

- Another nice sauce for this fish is "Salsa à la Pineapple."
- Serve with fresh vegetables to add some vibrant color.

Food and Water

*D*ear sisters, let's seriously assess how well we are taking care of ourselves nutritionally. All the food people brought us at first is long gone. It is easy to just grab something, anything, or even forget to eat. When Matt died, it was too hard to even chew, so I lived on smoothies and soup for a while.

Grief is exhausting and uses an enormous amount of energy. Our bodies need nutritious food to support us in this time of mourning. Have you tried the Yogurt Smoothies or Comforting Noodles or Elegant Chicken?

In our Western culture, we tend to think of our bodies as something separate from our minds. Yet we are actually one integrated, whole organism and we will be better able to cope with the sadness if we can take care of our whole selves.

Health researchers say that grief, stress, and depression experienced by widows and widowers make them more likely to eat comfort foods and fast-food meals in place of more nutritious options. (Think pizza, sandwiches, French fries, soft drinks, convenience meals, etc.) You probably know that a steady diet of these inevitably leads to cardiovascular illnesses. (See more in Fagundes article in the References.)

Look in your refrigerator and throw away anything that looks old and tired or unappealing. Getting rid of old food and replacing it with fresh things that appeal to you is an investment in healing.

We have permission to buy, cook and eat things that perhaps our mate didn't like. This can open up new possibilities for good nutrition for us.

Along with nutritious food, we must drink water throughout the day. Add a slice of cucumber or lemon wedge to a fresh glass of water to make it more appealing. Sparkling water counts! These things—nutritious food and water—will make a big difference in how we feel and how much energy we have to deal with what we are going through.

- What were their favorite foods?
- What differences did you have in food likes and dislikes?
- What new dishes would you like to try?

Steak Salad with Cranberry Vinaigrette

Not only does this taste really, really good, but the salad is low carb.

Ingredients	Directions
2 tsp. canola or other neutral oil, divided 1 small strip steak (about 8 oz.) 2 cups lightly packed salad greens 1/2 small cucumber, thinly sliced $1/3$ cup shredded carrots $1/3$ cup red onion thinly sliced 1 T. fresh cilantro, chopped (dressing ingredients on next page)	1. Slice strip steak into ¼ inch slices, cutting against the grain. 2. Heat 2 tsp. of oil in deep non-stick skillet or wok on medium-high heat. Stir-fry beef to desired doneness. (It will continue to cook a little even after removal from pan.) (See air-fryer option below.) 3. To make dressing, in small bowl, whisk together all ingredients until blended.

3 T. cranberry juice cocktail

2 T. cider vinegar

1 tsp. Dijon mustard

1 tsp. canola oil

¼ tsp. ground ginger

⅛ tsp. sugar

¼ tsp. water

4. Make up two individual bowls of salad each with greens, cucumber, carrots, red onions, and cilantro.
5. To one of the bowls, add dressing as desired and then half of the steak slices. (Save the other bowl for later or tomorrow.)
6. Enjoy with either warm or cold steak.

Notes

- Cover and refrigerate the second bowl of lettuce. Store dressing separately and mix when ready to eat.
- The dressing recipe makes enough to dress 3 or 4 salads.
- Air fryer option: Steak may also be cooked in an air-fryer, 6 minutes per side for medium, allowed to rest 10 minutes, then sliced.
- If you like to grill your steaks, that works great too for this recipe.

Boundaries & Invitations

*D*ear sisters, I hope you are blessed with thoughtful, loving friends who comfort and support you. Sometimes, however, well-meaning friends can be unhelpful. This includes giving unrequested advice, telling us what we should or shouldn't be feeling or doing, or giving patently wrong information. Pressuring us to go to events we don't feel up to yet is usually done with good intentions but can be distressing.

Assuming our friends have good intentions to help us, here are some handy phrases to have at the ready:

- Thanks for worrying about me, but I have to do this my own way.
- It will work better for me if I ….
- What would really help is if you could… "Pick up a bag of coffee for me."
- Thank you for inviting me. I can't join you right now. Very sorry to miss it.
- I'm sorry I won't be able to join you. Hopefully in the future when I feel up to it.
- I can't do it right now.

Long-term isolation isn't healthy either. Aim for a balance of time alone and time with people. We all need some of each. Grief is exhausting and we need rest. Accept invitations when you are ready and have the energy.

- How successful are you at setting comfortable boundaries with friends, family members, yourself?
- What is your optimal balance between alone time and time with others?
- What do you need to do differently going forward?

Riffs on Rice

Rice does not have to be boring!

Soothing Rice

Ingredients	Directions
½ cup long grain rice 1 cup broth—vegetable, mushroom, or chicken ¼ tsp. salt Butter Parmesan cheese, grated (to taste)	1. Place rice in small, heavy-bottomed pot. Add broth and salt. Bring to a boil. 2. When rice is boiling vigorously, turn the heat way down so that the rice is simmering gently. Put the lid on. 3. Cook over low heat for 15 minutes. 4. Remove from heat and let stand for 5 minutes. 5. Fluff with a fork and add one T. butter and as much Parmesan cheese as you wish.

Green Rice

Ingredients	Directions

½ cup long grain rice
1 cup broth—vegetable,
  mushroom, or chicken
¼ tsp. salt
Handful of fresh spinach,
  chopped,
or 1 heaping T. fresh
  parsley, chopped
	1. Cook rice as directed
	   above through Step 3.
	2. Before taking pot off
	   the heat, mix in fresh
	   spinach or parsley.
	3. Let stand for five min-
	   utes.

Brown Rice

Use brown rice for any recipes above if desired. For one serving of brown rice, combine 2/3 cup of rinsed brown rice to 1 and ⅓ cups water or broth, and ¼ tsp. of salt to a small heavy-bottomed pot. Bring to a boil, cover, and cook slowly for 45-60 minutes. Check to be sure water has not boiled away and add more if needed.

Notes

Keep Moving

*D*ear sisters, for many of us, it feels impossible to even think about exercising. As grievers, we are more tired than usual. We may have muscle and joint aches in addition to the emotional pain. We may be more accident prone. And we are sad. These things are not conducive to heading over to the gym to exercise. So let's forget about exercise altogether and think simply about moving our bodies.

Staying sedentary can make us feel worse, but regular physical movement can help us cope with those very symptoms of grief. As you may know, exercise stimulates the release of natural mood lifters and stress reducers. For some people, movement works as well as medication for depression according to Harvard Medical School.

For those of us who haven't been able to move our body much, we can start today by just walking to the mailbox or to the corner. Take it slow. Write down your walking minutes in this book. That walk to the mailbox can soon increase to a 5-minute walk, then to 10 minutes, then 15 minutes, then 20 minutes. Evidence exists now that just 20 minutes per day of walking has health benefits for improving mood, heart health, mental sharpness, immune system response and weight management. I have had good luck aiming for a morning and an evening walk, each only 10 minutes each.

Other gentle forms of exercise include Tai Chi, Qi Gong, and Yoga. And don't forget dancing! You don't need anyone else around to dance if you feel like it.

35

Walking indoors on a treadmill is great movement too, but we miss out on the benefits of the fresh air and vitamin D from the sun.

Taking a workout class with a friend or having a walking buddy helps us get out the door. And really that is the hardest part. People who had a very intense exercise program prior to their loss, however, are encouraged to take it slow and easy in early grief.

An added bonus of committing to moving each day is that it is something we have control over. When so much in our lives is out of our control, it's empowering to make this healthy choice for ourselves.

- What are you doing now to move your body every day?
- What physical movement are you willing to commit to doing every day?
- How will you keep track of your activity?

No-Fuss Chicken Noodle Soup

*What is more comforting than a
bowl of hot chicken soup?*

Ingredients	Directions

2 tsp. olive oil
½ cup celery, diced small
½ cup onion, diced small
¼ cup carrot, diced small
2 cups good quality
  chicken broth
¼ cup dry white wine
  (optional)
Uncooked boneless,
  skinless chicken breast
  (8-10 oz.)
2 oz. angel hair pasta
  broken into 1-inch
  pieces (See Notes
  below)
2 T. fresh parsley or dill,
  chopped
Salt and Pepper to taste
Squeeze of lemon
  (optional)
	1. Heat oil is a large pot on medium-high heat.
	2. Sauté celery, onion, and carrot until celery and onions are starting to soften, but are still crisp (3-5 minutes).
	3. Give it a few shakes of salt and pepper.
	4. Add broth and water and wine (if using) and bring to a boil.
	5. Add chicken breast, reduce to a simmer and cover.
	6. Simmer until chicken is cooked through— about 10 minutes. It should register 165° F. on meat thermometer.

7. Remove chicken with tongs and chop into bite-sized pieces.
8. Add pasta to pot and cook until tender, about 4 minutes.
9. Stir in chicken and parsley/dill. Add salt and pepper if needed. A squeeze of lemon will give it brightness, but it is optional.

Notes

- You can use leftover rotisserie chicken for this recipe. Since it is already cooked, add it last and just heat it through.
- For measuring 2 oz. of angel hair if you don't have a food scale: Hold a small bunch of pasta in your hand. A 2-ounce bunch should be as big around as a U.S. quarter.

Re-entry

*D*ear sisters, at some point, we will want to or have to venture out of our pain bubble. We might feel a desire to do some "normal" things. At the same time, consider that it is not possible right now to do all the things we did before, at least not in the same way. We need to take re-entry in small steps.

Here are a few suggestions for re-entry.

- Think about what you can stop doing at home for now.
- Simplify your daily routine as much as you can.
- Start with short hours or days at work.
- Talk to your boss to ensure that the most important things get done.
- Talk to your work team about your schedule and workload.
- Let co-workers and friends know if you want to talk about your loved one.
- Tell stories and share your memories.
- Take a temporary break from committee or volunteer work.
- Hang out with positive people.
- Avoid toxic people.
- Avoid multi-tasking if possible.
- Remember to eat, sleep, and move your body.
- Spend some time getting spiffed up—it can lift your spirits.

In a nutshell, consider that you are a different person than before losing your life partner. For now, just do what you can.

- What do you look forward to as you return to your work or usual routine?
- What do you think will be the hardest thing for you in going back?
- What suggestions from the list above would help you?

Baked Salmon

Worthy of a dinner party!

Ingredients	Directions
Two salmon fillets (4-5 oz. each) 1 T. plus 1 tsp. olive oil 2 tsp. lemon juice 2 tsp. fresh parsley, chopped 1 large clove of garlic, minced 1 tsp. dried basil (or 1 T. fresh basil leaves, chopped) 1 tsp. ground ginger (or 2 tsp. fresh ginger, finely chopped) Pinch of cayenne pepper (optional) Lemon wedges	1. Preheat oven to 400° 2. Whisk together all ingredients except the salmon. 3. Place salmon on a baking sheet lined with parchment paper for easy cleanup. 4. Spoon the herb mixture onto the salmon, coating top and sides. 5. Bake 9-12 minutes. 6. Serve with lemon wedges.

Notes

What's Comforting?

*D*ear sisters, we need all the comfort we can get. At first, I felt the best when I was with a small group of friends who knew and loved Matt. We got together every Friday night, giving me a reprieve from the pain and a chance to talk about Matt with those special people who cared about him.

Another outlet for my grief was trying new recipes. My aim was to try a new recipe each week. I wasn't really interested in eating the results, but I did love experimenting with different ingredients. I shared my recipe creations with friends and family.

Taking myself to a movie gave me a two-hour break to get mentally immersed in something other than pain. I took an online exercise class which kept me very busy for an hour—another break from the pain circuit. I took time to meditate, focusing on attention to my breathing. Massage appointments helped body and soul. Writing to him every night was probably the most comforting of all. If there was ever a time to find little things that give us comfort, it is now.

Other comforting strategies could be these:

- A warm bath with lovely fragrances.
- Scented candles or other aromatherapy.
- A warm blanket.
- A weighted blanket.
- A new haircut, manicure, or pedicure.
- An audio book to listen to with your feet up and your eyes closed.

- What provides the most comfort for you in this time of grief?
- How can you get more of that?

Peach Crisp

Sweet treatment for those chin-drippin'
peaches of summer.

Ingredients	Directions
1 and ⅓ cups sliced and peeled peaches (about 2 peaches) 2 tsp. lime juice or lemon juice 2 T. brown sugar Pinch of cinnamon 2 T. Flour 1 T. white sugar 1 T. cold butter 2 T. chopped nuts	1. Preheat oven to 350° F. 2. Toss together peaches, juice, brown sugar, and cinnamon. 3. Place in a small, buttered baking dish or ramekin (2-cup capacity). 4. Combine flour and white sugar, then cut in butter with a pastry blender or two table knives so that butter is in pea-sized pieces. 5. Sprinkle flour/butter mixture over the peaches, then sprinkle with the nuts.

6. Bake 35-45 minutes or until the peaches are cooked through, the juices are bubbling, and the topping is lightly browned.

Notes

- Place dish or ramekin on a cookie sheet to bake as the peach mixture may bubble out.

Grief Fog

*D*ear sisters, we are not alone in feeling disoriented and bewildered. The famous writer, Joan Didion, describes how her mind just couldn't take in the death of her husband. She tells of her "derangement" at his death, such as giving a long-past address for his death certificate.

She describes readying his clothing and shoes to be donated. As she looked at the shoes, she writes, "I could not give away the rest of his shoes. I stood there for a moment, then realized why: he would need shoes if he was to return." (From *The Year of Magical Thinking.*)

I had similar illogical thoughts after Matt died. For a long time afterwards, I felt unconsciously that he had been gone long enough, that I had waited alone long enough, that it was time for him to come home. I knew my dear husband was dead and yet a part of me was waiting for him to come back.

In the first week after he died, I was so muddled that I found myself wondering if he had really lived or if I had just imagined this wonderful person. I still remember the worried look on my granddaughter's face when I said that out loud. I also found myself unable to drive my car.

Our minds can go to strange places when we are suffering. The common term for this is "grief fog." We need to be gentle with ourselves when we have illogical, crazy thoughts, worries, and reactions. We can always ask for a reality check from a trusted friend or professional therapist.

Knowing that disorientation and even denial is part of the grief journey, as we do our grief work, we can expect clearer days ahead.

- What fog, confusion, disorientation, illogical thoughts or actions have you experienced since the death of your beloved?
- What might a kind and loving friend say to you about these moments?
- What might your beloved tell you to do?

Poached Chicken Breast

Like the little black dress—dress it up or down.

Ingredients	Directions
1 boneless, skinless chicken breast (6-8 oz.) ½ tsp. kosher salt 1 bay leaf Water to cover **Choice of optional seasonings:** ½ cup dry white wine Garlic clove, smashed Fresh ginger slices Lemon slices Onion slices Fresh herbs Dried herbs Whatever seasoning you like	1. Add enough water to a saucepan so that it will ultimately cover the chicken breast by at least an inch. 2. Add salt, bay leaf, and any other seasonings you wish to use. 3. Bring water to a boil and then simmer, covered, for 5 minutes. 4. Add chicken to pan and reduce heat to low, cover, and simmer 8-12 minutes. (Do not let the chicken boil.) 5. Test for doneness (165°F.) with meat thermometer inserted in the thickest part of the meat. 6. Transfer chicken breast to a cutting board, cover, and let it rest for 10 minutes before slicing.

Notes

- If foam rises to the top of the poaching liquid while chicken cooks, it does not need to be skimmed off unless you plan to use the cooking liquid as a soup base. (The foam tends to make the broth cloudy.)
- If poaching chicken legs and/or thighs, aim for internal temperature of 175° to 190° F. An intact leg and thigh can take 30+ minutes to poach, depending on size.
- Skin may be left on or removed before poaching chicken legs and thighs.
- Add to soups or salads or use for traditional chicken salad or enchiladas or tacos or the humble sliced chicken sandwich.

Stuff and Belongings

*D*ear sisters, sooner or later we are faced with the decision about what to do with our beloved's clothes and all their "stuff." It's never easy. It can feel like we are getting rid of them, erasing the tangible proof of their lives. It's overwhelming. This is something to do only when we feel ready and on our own time schedule. There is no right or wrong way to do it.

One article advised that I should dispose of all my husband's clothing in one day. That would have been impossible for me.

Another article suggested donating or giving to family members or selling things as it felt right. That is the approach I took. I still have some of his things because I have yet to decide what I will do with them. I will make these decisions, but on my own schedule. The perfect choice of who to give an item to will often just pop into my mind. I go with it.

On the other hand, we need room and space to redesign a life for ourselves. We don't owe it to our partner to keep all their things as a tribute to them. People in the community desperately need clothing and household items. Family members often want random personal items as keepsakes. (Equally as often, family members don't want a lot of additional things.) A legal will may direct certain things go to certain people. Asking trusted family or close friends to help with deciding these things is a very good idea.

We might have a general sequence in mind of what to focus on first such as medications, clothing, computers, books, knick-knacks, office supplies, jewelry, etc. But we can do it on our own timeline. Take photographs of special things before donating or disposing of them. Looking at the photos later on can be comforting.

I have taken great comfort in using things that were my husband's. I love to use his good pen. I am writing this book with his computer monitor and mouse. Any time I can use something that was his, I do so. It comforts me.

- What are most precious to you of all your loved one's belongings?
- What is it hardest for you to part with and why is it so?
- What is your next step in gifting, donating, selling, or disposing of things?

....

....

....

....

....

....

....

....

....

....

....

....

Lentil Soup

The gentle lentil—so comforting...

Ingredients	Directions
1 tsp. olive oil ½ cup onion, chopped ¼ cup carrot, finely chopped ½ cup celery, finely chopped ½ cup raw potato, cut into small cubes 1 garlic clove, minced Salt and pepper to taste 2 cups chicken or vegetable broth 2 tsp. brown sugar or molasses 1 cup canned lentils, rinsed and drained. 1 T. red wine vinegar 2 tsp. dry red wine Lemon wedges or plain Greek yogurt	1. Heat oil over medium heat in a medium saucepan. Add onion, carrot, celery, potato, garlic and a dash of salt and pepper. 2. Stir-fry till veggies begin to soften, 3-5 minutes. 3. Add broth and brown sugar or molasses and bring to a boil. Lower heat and cook for 5 minutes. 4. Add lentils and cook till thickened, 3-5 minutes. 5. Stir in vinegar, red wine if using, and salt and pepper to taste. Heat through. 6. Serve with a squeeze of lemon or a dollop of Greek yogurt in each bowl.

Notes

- Extra lentils left over can be added to salads or other soups.
- If you prefer to cook your own lentils from scratch, you won't have to soak them overnight. Rinse ⅓ cup of uncooked lentils and combine with about 3 cups of water in a heavy-bottomed pot. Bring to a boil, reduce heat, and simmer, uncovered 15-20 minutes.
- Add cooked beef or chicken to this soup at the end to make it even heartier.
- This soup freezes very well.

Confidence Lost

Yesterday was a better day.
For a brief time I felt something like the old me...
instead of this sad stranger living in my skin.
It didn't last, of course.
By this morning the feeling of "better" had gone....
But still, for those few hours,
it gave a glimpse of the possibility
that there could be other days to come
that would be better,
other days where I would again feel
somewhat like Me.

Helen Reichert Lambin

*D*ear sisters, of the many things I could not have known about grieving for Matt was how worthless and inept I would feel. It made no sense. I had been through the excruciating experience of losing him. Why did I lose my own self-confidence?

I was no longer able to function professionally for a long time, a huge blow for me, a management consultant. Thus, I found myself also grieving the loss of my professional credibility. It didn't help that I couldn't drive at first—I was literally afraid to get behind the wheel at first because I was so disoriented. I was Mr. Magoo.

I have learned that grieving people commonly find their self-confidence and self-esteem destroyed by grief. But why is it so common to feel bad about ourselves, insufficient, even worthless after experiencing our loss?

These personal doubts are directly related to how much the person meant to us. We had joined our life to theirs. Although we were separate, we were one. That "one" was cut in half leaving us "eviscerated" as one man described it.

We are grieving so many things at the same time—not just the loss of that precious person, but the loss of the future life we imagined, the loss of the daily life we had together, possibly the loss of friends, and often the loss of status and financial security. We know our life won't ever be the same. We are undone by it all.

When we recognize this, we can see we have a new challenge in front of us—to create a life that works for us in our new reality. Even, as a grieving friend suggested, to reinvent ourselves. This is not so easy, but it is achieved in small steps. Staying connected with our lost love in comforting ways, accepting how bad we feel, asking for help when we need it, doing things we have always wanted to do, trying new things when we have the energy, reaching out to friends, taking care of ourselves, and celebrating the ways in which we are strong and moving forward. All these things together can help us rebuild ourselves and reclaim our self-confidence.

- What strengths and abilities did your beloved admire and appreciate in *you*?
- In what ways do you feel *less* confident than you did before?
- In what ways might you feel *more* confident now?

Fork-Tender Pork Chops (Slow Cooker)

Tangy and tender and cooks while you nap.

Ingredients	Directions
2 boneless pork chops, trimmed 8 oz. tomato sauce 2 T. brown sugar 1 T. apple cider vinegar 2 tsp. Worcestershire sauce ½ tsp. salt 1½ T. olive oil ½ medium onion, sliced 1 medium green bell pepper, sliced	1. Whisk tomato sauce, brown sugar, vinegar, Worcestershire sauce and salt in a bowl. 2. Heat olive oil on "browning" setting in slow cooker (or place in a skillet over medium heat). 3. Brown pork chops in hot oil about 5 minutes per side. 4. Place onion and green pepper on top of pork chops in slow cooker. 5. Pour tomato sauce mixture into slow cooker, gently stirring. 6. Cook on low heat until tender, 6-8 hours.

Notes
- Serve with couscous, quinoa, rice, or mashed potatoes.

Time Alone

Dear sisters, just as everyone experiences grief in their own way, we all have vastly different experiences and views around being alone. If we have no children at home and no parents or relatives to care for, we could be alone for weeks at a time. For a young mother who has lost her children's father or step-father, there probably isn't any alone time.

Which scenario is healthier? Well, neither is ideal.

Many people naturally turn inward in grief. Being alone gives us the time to try to absorb what has happened, to feel how we feel, to shed the tears, to wail in private. Given the profound emotional, physical, and spiritual impacts of losing a partner, we may not have the energy to interact much with other people, especially in the early days. Solitude can be a welcome space.

Yet too much time alone is not helpful for moving through grief and is actually a health hazard. Grief writer Rachel Kodanaz suggests that if we spend more than two-thirds of the waking day alone [say 10 hours out of a 15-hour day], we need to add more time spent in the company of others, even if it's only one extra hour each day.

Those of us who live alone particularly need to stay aware of how much time we spend in isolation. If we shut out other people and the rest of the world, we delay our own healing. As humans, we need the support and love of other people, especially now.

Some grievers, on the other hand, avoid their pain and sadness by distracting themselves with constant social engagements, events, trips, nonstop television and radio noise, and busyness, ensuring they will not have to spend any time alone in sadness. Avoiding alone time typically prolongs the healing process. Sooner or later, the pain demands to be dealt with.

To move forward in our grief work, we need a healthy balance between quiet times of solitude and time spent with others. What ideal balance looks like is unique to each of us.

- What is your usual attitude towards being alone?
- Do you have adequate time these days to turn inward, to be with your grief? If not, how might you find or create that time?
- Do you have adequate opportunities these days to be with other people? If not, how might you find or create that time?

Real Ranch Dressing

*Once you make this dressing, you won't
like the stuff from the grocery store.*

Ingredients	Directions
⅔ cup buttermilk ½ cup mayonnaise 2 tsp. Worcestershire sauce ½ tsp. onion powder ½ tsp. onion flakes ¼ tsp. garlic powder 1 T. fresh chives, chopped 1 T. fresh dill, chopped 1 T. fresh parsley, chopped ½ tsp. kosher salt ¼ tsp pepper	1. Whisk together buttermilk, mayonnaise, Worcestershire, onion powder, onion flakes, and garlic powder. 2. Add chives, dill, and parsley. Season with salt and pepper (more or less to taste). Mix all well.

Notes
- This dressing keeps well in the refrigerator for at least two weeks.

Money Matters

Dear sisters, as if losing our beloved companion isn't enough to bear, financial questions can arise while we are in the painful fog of grief. Most grief writers recommend that, if possible, we not make major financial decisions before at least a year has passed after a partner's death.

Decisions to sell our home, move to a different community, buy or sell stocks and bonds, and cash-in IRAs and annuities usually have long-term consequences. In the early days of grief, we are not in mental or emotional shape to make these kinds of decisions. Given time, we will be able to make them.

For most people, the loss of a life-partner is also a loss of half or more of their income. This can ignite a panic response and emotion-based decisions that might not be ideal. Making these decisions too soon can impose even more stress. For example, imagine trying to clean out, repair, and spruce up a home to sell; then find a new place to live; and finally packing up to move, broken-hearted and exhausted with grief. Other options may exist, but we will need time to figure that out.

Aim for keeping things *status quo* in the short term. As suggested earlier in this book, we can ask someone we trust to help with the barrage of mail to ensure at least the bills get paid on time.

We will need professional financial advice for the long term so we can know our options and the pros and cons of various choices down the road. This should happen sometime in the first year so we know where we stand financially. What made financial sense for us as a couple might not be right for us now. You may or may not wish to continue with the same financial advisor you had together.

Unfortunately, anyone can call themselves a financial planner. I like to know that my financial advisor is a Certified Financial Planner® as this ensures they have met professional standards. Friends and family may be able to suggest reliable professionals such as accountants or attorneys for you to work with. Regardless of who we choose to work with, we do need to check their credentials and reputation before making a commitment.

When Matt died, a family friend who is very savvy with investing and all things financial helped me get a handle on my financial picture. He drew a picture for me of the various income sources and investments and liabilities which had just been spaghetti to me. I can't tell you how many times I looked at that simple diagram. When I met with my new financial advisor, I was so much more knowledgeable and confident. I am glad I didn't try to figure it all out alone.

- What are your biggest financial questions right now?
- Who could help you sort your finances in the short term?

Summer Couscous Salad

Crunchy and chewy, yet tender—perfect for a cookout.

Ingredients	Directions
⅓ cup water Pinch of dried thyme 5 T. plus 1 tsp. uncooked couscous (the instant type) ¼ cup green bell pepper, chopped ¼ cup tomato, peeled, seeded, and chopped 2 T. "Real Ranch Dressing" (from previous entry) or bottled creamy cucumber dressing 1 T. raisins, chopped 1 tsp. fresh lemon juice (optional) 2 tsp. fresh chives, minced 1 T. roasted, unsalted peanuts, chopped	1. Combine water and thyme in a small saucepan and bring to a boil. 2. Remove from heat and add couscous. 3. Cover and let stand 5 minutes or until the couscous is tender and the liquid is absorbed. Fluff with a fork. 4. Add green pepper, tomato, raisins, chives, lemon juice if using, and dressing. Mix well. 5. Transfer mixture to a serving bowl, cover and chill. 6. Just before serving, top with the chopped peanuts.

Notes

- Add half of a 15 oz. can of black-eyed peas or other beans in Step 4 to boost the protein in this dish.
- Most of the couscous you find at the grocery store will be the instant kind with the very brief prep time described above. The grains will be very small, smaller than a grain of rice.

Dark Thoughts

One of the most important parts of grief work
is moving from wanting to die to wanting to live,
to come home to oneself
no matter how different that self is now.

Jan Warner

*D*ear sisters, it is easy to wonder if life is even worth living when we are in the depths of grief. Or to feel we can't go on living without our partner. It's a common feeling.

Many grievers who wonder how they can live without their lost partner feel ashamed and embarrassed. They might feel like weaklings or sinners for having those feelings and thoughts, and thus be reluctant to disclose them to anyone. The feeling that we cannot live anymore without our mates is not quite the same as actively considering suicide, but the figures bear out that thinking about taking our own life or at least not caring of we live is more common than most of us realize.

Some people stop living while they're alive. They lose energy, become unmotivated, and give up altogether. All of these feelings can lead to a downward spiral of depression. It's not surprising studies bear out that suicidal ideation is higher among widowed people than married people.

Silence is not strength. If we are having thoughts of self-harm, disengageament, or suicide, then is the time to connect with a professional. Call 988 anywhere in the United States at any time of the day or night or use the chat on this website https://988lifeline.org/. You can count on a friendly voice and understanding chat.

Grief writer David Kessler suggests that to rebuild our life we switch from thinking "I will never live again" to "I will live a life to honor my loved one."

Another strategy suggested by grief writers Eleanor Haley and Litsa Williams is to make a list of reasons to live or things worth living for. They say this is helpful even for grievers who haven't experienced thoughts of not wanting to live any longer. The list is intended not to resolve the pain but to remind us that—even though we have darkness in our lives—we also can have light and goodness.

- Name *specific* things in your life worth living for (names, places, events).

Tangy Chicken Thighs (Slow Cooker)

This smells so good as it cooks.
It's hard to wait till it's done.

Ingredients	Directions
2 chicken thighs, bone-in, skin-on ½ cup shallots, sliced (or mild onion) 4 cloves garlic, crushed 6 T. soy sauce (regular or low-sodium) ¼ cup red wine vinegar	1. Place chicken in slow cooker. 2. Mix shallot, garlic, soy sauce and vinegar in a small bowl and pour over the chicken. 3. Cook on Low for 5 hours. Meat thermometer should read at least 175° F. for chicken thighs.

Notes
- Serve with brown or white rice, quinoa, or couscous.
- If you have a larger slow cooker, say 6 quart capacity, consider getting a smaller one, 2-3 quart size, for your everyday meals. Save the big one for family events and potlucks.

The Grief Journey

Healing is an active process.
We have to decide if we want to live again....
It's a commitment.

David Kessler

Dear sisters, it's a journey no one wants to take. One writer says grief shouldn't even be spoken of as a journey because it's about yearning and pain and adjustment, not travel. It's sure not like taking a cruise.

I think, however, that "grief journey" describes well what we are going through. Like any journey, grief has a starting point. For us, it was a diagnosis, or accident, or death. Like all journeys, it changes us. We learn things, see things, experience new feelings, gain new insights, and maybe even get lost once or twice.

The destination for grief is not the absence of longing or love. Our destination is arriving at a place where our love warms and illuminates our lives and we actually do have a fulfilling life on our own. We can reach a point where we can appreciate and enjoy the life we have been given. This takes time, and honestly, some effort on our part. It can be hard to imagine in the early months of grief, but that is the journey—from loss to finding meaning in our own precious lives. Safe travels!

- Describe the "destination" you hope to reach in your grief journey.
- What might it feel like; what will you be doing?
- Who else is involved?

One-Banana Bread

For that one last lonely left-over banana.

Ingredients	Directions
⅓ cup white sugar 2 T. canola oil 1 egg yolk 1 ripe banana, mashed 2 T. sour cream or plain Greek yogurt ½ tsp. vanilla ½ cup plus 2 T. flour ¼ tsp. baking soda Pinch of cinnamon ⅛ tsp. salt	1. Preheat oven to 350° F. 2. Grease small loaf pan. 3. In a small bowl, stir together sugar, oil, and banana. 4. Add in egg, sour cream (or yogurt), and vanilla. Stir to combine. 5. Add in flour, baking soda, cinnamon, and salt. Mix until just combined. (Do not overmix.) 6. Pour into pan and bake for 30-35 minutes or until a toothpick inserted comes out clean. 7. Cool for 5 minutes and then remove from pan and cool completely.

Notes

Grieving the Past

Love came first.

Donna Ashworth

Dear sisters, we long for everything to be like it used to be when we had the love and support of our living partner. We miss the vacations, dinners, holidays, private jokes, physical intimacy, text messages, calls, getting picked up at the airport, walking the dog or shopping for groceries together, holding hands, hugs, the great relief of being totally ourselves with another person.

We grieve over the things we wish we would have said and the things we wish we had not said. And the one thing that could make us feel better, the return of our beloved life companion, is the one thing we know we cannot have.

Grief is the signature of love given and received. If you are grieving, you experienced love. As much as you are hurting now, you know you wouldn't have missed your life together.

- What times and experiences with your beloved will you always remember?
- What was the *single* best part of your life together?

Tuna Pasta Salad

This refreshing salad is a picnic all by itself.

Ingredients	Directions
1 T. white wine vinegar ¼ cup plus 1 T. extra virgin olive oil 1 ¼ tsp kosher salt, divided 4 oz. elbow pasta 5-oz. can of tuna (water-packed, drained) 1 T. shallots or mild onion, finely chopped ¼ cup celery, finely chopped ¼ cup green pepper, finely chopped ¼ tsp. ground black pepper 1 T. fresh basil, chopped **Garnish:** lemon wedges cherry tomatoes, thinly sliced cucumber, thinly sliced	1. Pour vinegar into a medium bowl and slowly whisk in olive oil. 2. Bring a large pot of water to boil and add 1 tsp. kosher salt. 3. Stir the pasta into the boiling water and cook according to package directions (less about 1 minute). 4. Drain pasta in a strainer and shake to remove extra water from elbows. 5. Pour pasta into a large bowl. Gently stir in tuna, shallots, celery, green pepper, black pepper, ¼ tsp. kosher salt, basil.

	6. Gently blend in vinegar and oil dressing.
	7. Garnish as desired.
	8. Refrigerate until ready to serve.

Notes

- Spring-time green peas are nice in this salad and they don't even have to be cooked.
- If you only have strong onions rather than the milder shallots on hand, you can soak the onions in cold water for 5-10 minutes and then dry well with paper towels to make them less pungent.

Rituals and Ceremonies

Ritual is a way of putting a pin
in the map of our lives
and saying
"this matters."

Jessie Harrold

*D*ear sisters, rituals and ceremonies say more than words alone. They can ground us at a time when life feels chaotic. And a ritual shared with other people helps keep us connected with them rather than isolated in our grief.

Our family has a ritual each year on Matt's birthday where we all meet up at a beautiful point on the University of Wisconsin-Madison campus—Picnic Point on Lake Mendota. All of us, including babies and children, walk out to the point and back. Along the way we reminisce about times when we were together on Matt's boat or stop at points where we used to anchor the boat and swim over to the sandy beach. Then we meet up for a picnic where each family brings whatever they wish to eat, so no one has to worry about food for a crowd. We sit in a circle in our lawn chairs and enjoy our picnic and enjoy being together. I always feel that Matt is with us.

Another lovely ceremony is coming together to plant a tree in honor of our beloved. Trees, by themselves, are a universal symbol of life. A tree is a permanent memorial that will hopefully flourish far into the future. You might want to have a short reading or reflection to begin the ceremony and end it after the tree has been planted. A metal memorial plaque can be placed as part of the ceremony.

Another option is to have a memorial tree (or grove of trees) planted by the Arbor Day Foundation or similar organization.

A candle-lighting ceremony can be done anywhere. A center candle is set out and lit. A small group of family and friends stands in a circle. Each person holds their own small candle. One by one, each person lights their memory candle and shares a special memory. When all the candles have been lit and memories shared, a song may be sung, a poem read, a prayer offered, or a few moments of silent reflection observed.

Every year, our family observes Matt's *birthday* together rather than the anniversary of his death, which we usually observe in our own way. I think it's a good thing because his death was such a small part of his life—one moment in time compared to the full life he lived and compared to everything Matt continues to mean to us.

- What kind of ritual or ceremony with family and friends in honor of your life companion might give you comfort at this point?
- What ritual or ceremony in honor of your beloved could you do on your own, at your own pace, as often—or as infrequently—as you choose?
- What ritual or ceremony *for you* might your beloved have approved of, and maybe held, if *you* had died first? Why do you think this?

Asparagus-Potato Soup

Light jade in color, silky, and hard to resist!

Ingredients	Directions
2 tsp. canola oil 3/4 cup fresh asparagus, chopped 1½ cups raw, peeled potatoes, diced small ¼ cup onions, chopped 1 rib celery, chopped ¼ tsp. salt 1½ cups chicken broth ½ cup milk (whole or low-fat) 1 tsp. lemon juice Dollop of sour cream or plain yogurt Bacon, cooked and crumbled Fresh parsley or dill Red pepper flakes Crumbled feta or Cotija cheese	1. Heat oil in small Dutch oven or heavy pan. 2. Sprinkle salt over the vegetables (asparagus, potatoes, onions, celery) and sauté together till starting to soften. 3. Add broth, cover, and cook on low heat for 20-30 minutes. (Potatoes should be falling apart when done.) 4. Add milk, stir, and heat through. (Do not boil.) 5. Blend until smooth with an immersion blender or carefully add to a food processor to blend.

6. Place lemon juice in a small cup. Add a T. of hot soup and stir. Add a few more tablespoons and stir. (This will prevent curdling.) Add this mixture to soup and stir.
7. If too thick, add more water, broth, or milk.
8. Garnish as desired.

Notes

- This soup is cooked "low and slow" because of the relatively small amount of liquid. Cooking too quickly or without a lid can cause the broth to evaporate instead of cooking the spuds.
- This soup can be made with vegetable broth as a vegetarian option. Additional broth, hot water, or nut or grain milks may be used for the lactose intolerant.

Love Letters

When we continue to talk and
communicate with our loved one,
we open ourselves to their presence
—whether real or imaginary is irrelevant—
and we open ourselves to their guidance.
Learning to talk, and listen, to our loved one
can be immensely comforting.

Noel & Blair

Dear sisters, after Matt died, I wrote to him every night. Several years later, I still write to him every night in a notebook to tell him about things that would have interested him and to pour out my heart to him. I even add photos I know he would enjoy. (I have filled many notebooks.) I tell him things I don't necessarily share with others. Here is a sample entry:

My love, sometimes when the pain of missing you is so bad and I am feeling sorry for myself, I think that you got the better end of the deal. You are no longer suffering. Then I remind myself that your life was cut short, but I still have my life and all it brings— full moons, family, creativity, coffee, love…and friendship and pain too. There is no point in comparing our fates. We got what we got, but I sure wish you were with me here.

By the way, I just heard that Bed Bath and Beyond is closing all its stores. I felt sorry to hear it. We used to have so much fun looking at all the cooking stuff together. More later.

XXOO

I am not delusional about this. I just know writing to my husband is very comforting for me. It reflects my reality, that I will never be the same without him, but it also reminds me that I treasure the part he played, and still plays, in my life.

- What thoughts would you like to share now with your beloved?
- What photographs or drawings would you like to share if you could? (If size permits, add one of them here.)

Poached Salmon with Cucumber Sauce

Salmon poached in a small ocean of broth.
And the sauce, oh my!

Ingredients	Directions
½ medium cucumber, peeled and chopped ⅓ cup onion or shallot, finely chopped 1 T. red or white wine vinegar ¼ tsp. salt ¼ tsp. black pepper 1 T. fresh dill (about 2 sprigs) 4 oz. plain yogurt Two salmon filets (4-oz. each) 2 cups water or vegetable broth ½ cup dry white wine (optional) ½ lemon, sliced	1. Peel half a cucumber and cut in half lengthwise. Scrape out any seeds. Chop. 2. In a medium bowl, combine cucumber, onion, vinegar, salt and pepper. 3. Leave cucumber mixture covered at room temperature for 1 hour, stirring occasionally. 4. Drain cucumbers well and stir in dill and yogurt. Chill.

5. In a deep skillet or saucepan, bring water or stock, wine, and lemon slices to a boil. Reduce heat and simmer for 5 minutes.
6. Add salmon, cover, and gently simmer until just cooked through, about 9 minutes per inch of thickness. (Do not boil.)
7. Serve hot or cold with yogurt sauce and lemon wedges.

Notes
- Serve with white or brown rice.
- I have made the yogurt sauce when there wasn't time to let the cucumbers marinate, and it was still delicious.

Holidays

Missing them is remembering them.

Author unknown

*D*ear sisters, I don't have to tell you that holidays are a challenge for those of us who have lost a partner. We may dread a particular day that is coming up—national holidays or religious holidays like Thanksgiving, Christmas, New Years, Martin Luther King Day, Memorial Day, Fourth of July, Labor Day. Or special holidays like Kwanzaa, Easter, Eid, Yom Kippur, Holi—any holiday we once shared with our love.

Some of these holidays will hold more meaning for us than others, of course. Below are some things to think about and to do when dreading an upcoming holiday.

To Think About:

- You are not the same person now, so you cannot do everything you did before your loss.
- Sometimes dreading it is worse than the day itself.
- Although holidays may be hard, they can also include happy moments.
- You are not responsible for other people's holiday expectations. Others may be disappointed by your decisions, but they will survive.
- You can be alone without being lonely.
- After December 21, the days always get longer.

To Do:

- Stay with the day as it is. Resist the urge to compare your holiday now against those of the past.
- Make a list of what you are grateful for (or what you still have) during this holiday season.
- Let go of "should."
- Give yourself permission to change your mind, leave early, just pop in briefly, take care of yourself.
- Drive separately or call an Uber or Lyft so you control your time and location.
- If you don't feel up to the usual decorations, put out one or two or none.
- Make a donation in memory of your beloved.
- Keep it simple.
- Consider traveling on a holiday to visit friends or family, if you feel up to it.

Thanks to Eleanor Haley for several of these and additional suggestions for facing holidays.

- What upcoming holidays might be especially difficult for you this year?
- What strategies, if any, suggested on the previous page might help you cope today?

Salsa à la Pineapple

The Hawaiian shirt of salsas! Colorful,
bright and a little sassy.

Ingredients	Directions
1 cup fresh pineapple, diced 1 medium tomato, seeded and chopped ¼ cup shallot or sweet onion, chopped 1 heaping T. fresh cilantro, chopped 1 tsp. Jalapeño pepper, seeded and chopped (more if you like it hot) ½ T. extra virgin olive oil ⅛ tsp. ground coriander ⅛ tsp. ground cumin ¼ tsp. salt	1. Combine all ingredients. 2. Cover and refrigerate.

Notes

- I use disposable food prep gloves when cutting and seeding Jalapeños.
- Onions can be toned down by soaking in ice water for 5-10 minutes, then drained well and dried.
- To easily remove the tomato skin if desired, place the tomato in boiling water for a minute or two or until the skin starts peeling off, then plunge it into cold water and remove skin.
- Luscious served over rotisserie chicken or grilled fish and/or with tortilla chips.

Guilt & Regret

Would'a, Could'a, Should'a

*D*ear sisters, so many of us carry deep and/or unconscious feelings that we could have or should have done something different, that we are somehow responsible or partly responsible for what happened to our mate. After all, we are the ones who are still alive.

Or perhaps we regret that we had argued and not had the chance to mend. Maybe we had been overwhelmed with work and kids. Maybe we had forgotten to appreciate them. Or maybe we didn't realize how ill they were.

Many, many people carry plain old garden-variety survivor guilt—Why am I alive when my partner is dead? Although guilt and regret are not exactly the same thing, they feel the same—horrible.

These feelings of guilt and regret are part and parcel of grief. After all, you wouldn't have the big grief if you hadn't had the big love. It is helpful to get the regrets out in the open so they can be acknowledged and dealt with rather than pushed down.

A therapist or grief group can help you express and move through feelings of guilt and regret. You can also write a loving letter expressing your regrets and what you wish you could have done differently. Then write what you imagine and/or hope they would say back to you.

Dear _____

I would like to tell you _____

I am sorry _____

I wish I had _____

I hope you will _____

I hope you know_____

Then write what your beloved might say to *you* right now:

Dear _____

I would like to tell you _____

I am sorry _____

I wish I had _____

I hope you will _____

I hope you know_____

Mashed Potato

The ultimate comfort food—fluffy and satisfying.

Ingredients	Directions
1½ cups peeled, uncooked, cubed Russet or baking potato (about 1 big potato) Water to cover potato cubes Salt to taste 1 T. milk 2 tsp. soft butter Freshly ground black pepper 1 T. sour cream (Optional) Fresh parsley	1. Place potatoes in saucepan and cover with water salted to taste. 2. Boil potatoes until they are cooked through (they will fall off a fork) about 15 minutes. 3. Drain off water and mash potatoes with a masher or fork. 4. Add milk—more may be needed based on moisture in the potatoes. 5. Add butter, and sour cream, if using. 6. Add salt, pepper, milk, and parsley to taste.

Notes
- Whipping potatoes with a mixer can make them gummy, so best not to do that if avoidable.
- Yukon Gold potatoes may also be used.

Laughter

Do not make the mistake of living in sadness,
or living small to honor their absence.
You owe it to them to live even more vividly than before.
If they could reach you, they would surely say,
"Take the love you had for me and turn it into gladness...."

Donna Ashworth

Dear sisters, we can feel like we will never be able to laugh again. I remember the first time I laughed after Matt's death. At his celebration of life, a friend reminded me of something hilarious that had happened to us. I shocked myself by bursting out in a loud guffaw. My first thought was of guilt. How can I laugh at a time like this? I wondered if others thought this was undignified. But I also remember how good it felt to laugh.

One of the things I loved about Matt was that he had such a wicked sense of humor. I still laugh out loud when I think of some of the funny things he said. It gave me such joy to make him laugh as well.

When you laugh, not only is your mental load lightened, but it actually causes chemical changes in your body, such as stimulation of heart, lungs, and muscles and an increase in endorphins, the feel-good hormones. Relaxation and stress reduction follow a good laugh.

Chances are, we haven't been doing a lot of laughing lately, but let's give ourselves permission to watch silly YouTube videos or movie comedies we enjoyed in the past or to read things that make us chuckle. (I love *Mr. Bean* on PBS.)

Get together with a friend who has a great sense of humor. Laughter is healing and something our loved one would want for us.

- What funny events or situations or jokes did you and your life companion share? What made (and makes) these so humorous?
- What can you do now to bring more laughter into your life?
- Would your beloved approve? Why do you think so?

Garbanzo Sandwich Spread

Smoked paprika gives this sammich spread its zip.

Ingredients	Directions
¾ cup of canned garbanzo beans (cooked, no-salt-added), drained ¼ cup celery, finely chopped 1 green onion thinly sliced, white and green parts or 1 T. shallot, finely chopped 1 T. mayonnaise ½ tsp. Dijon prepared mustard 1 tsp. white wine vinegar ¼ tsp. Spanish smoked paprika Kosher salt and pepper to taste Lemon wedge Sliced olives	1. Place garbanzo beans in a medium bowl and smash them with a pastry blender or potato masher or fork until most are broken down. 2. Add celery and green onion and blend. 3. In a separate bowl, mix mayonnaise, mustard, wine vinegar, paprika, salt and pepper. 4. Pour mayo mixture over beans and gently combine. Garnish with lemon/olives. 5. Serve as a sandwich spread on whole grain bread or as a salad on shredded lettuce.

Notes

- Add the remaining garbanzo beans from a 15.5 oz can to salads or soups for added protein.
- If you prefer to cook the garbanzo beans yourself from scratch, use 1/4 cup of dry beans and soak overnight.
- Smoked paprika makes all the difference in this recipe.
- The kosher salt is not needed if you are using canned beans that contain salt.

Hard to Breathe

*D*ear sisters, when we are under stress, we naturally breathe faster and more shallowly. And what can be more stressful than losing the person we love?

Under stress, our brain and nervous system react as if we are under attack by a grizzly bear or other menace. We are on continual and largely unconscious high alert. The stress response speeds up our breathing so our lungs don't fill fully with air. Sometimes in our grief, just continuing to breathe at all can feel like a chore.

Shallow breathing is not physically or mentally good for us, especially now. We need more oxygen, not less, just to keep going. When stress hormones flood our bodies, blood pressure rises, our immune system is compromised and we are more anxious and depressed. Not only are we flooded with harmful hormones under stress, but the feel-good hormones like serotonin and dopamine are actually suppressed. We can, however, counteract some of these stress effects. Try this—

- Put your hands on your stomach and take a slow deep breath in through your nose to the count of four,
- Hold it for another count of four, and then,
- Slowly exhale through your mouth to a count of six.

You should have felt your stomach rise a bit as the air got to the lowest part of your lungs. Guess what else happened? Your brain exchanged a message with the rest of your body: "Don't worry. Things are OK. No grizzly bear here." The very opposite of a stress response.

Deep breathing releases endorphins, oxytocin, and serotonin which relaxes the body and mind. The fresh oxygen is distributed to all of our cells, providing new energy and helping all our organs function more optimally.

In the past, when I was upset and someone told me to "just breathe deeply," I was so annoyed—as if that could solve my problems. But using deep breathing as a tool helped me survive the worst days. I found it especially useful at night to get to sleep.

We can find all kinds of breathing and meditation exercises online, but really, just following the 4 x 4 x 6 sequence above can do wonders. Try for five minutes in a place where you won't be disturbed. Lying down or sitting up, eyes open or closed—whatever feels most comfortable.

- What *physical sensations* do you notice when you deepen your breathing?
- What *feelings* do you notice in deep breathing?
- What is the best *time and place* for you to do deep breathing?

Chicken & Zucchini Skillet

A perfect meal for Autumn, when the veggies are so beautiful and abundant.

Ingredients	Directions
1 T. olive oil 1 chicken breast (6-8 oz.) cubed in 2" pieces ½ cup onion, cut into wedges 1 garlic clove, chopped fine 1 zucchini (6-8 inches) 1 cup fresh tomato, chopped 1 tsp. fresh basil, chopped (or ¼ tsp. dried) 1 tsp. fresh oregano, chopped (or ¼ tsp. dried) ½ tsp. red pepper flakes (or to taste) Salt and pepper to taste Parmesan cheese, finely grated Lemon wedges	1. Heat a large skillet and add olive oil. Heat oil till shimmering. 2. Add chicken and brown lightly on all sides (about 10 minutes). 3. Add onion, garlic, and zucchini and stir fry for a few minutes. 4. Add tomato, basil, and oregano, and red pepper flakes. Stir. 5. Simmer, covered, over low heat 5-7 minutes or until vegetables are crisp-tender. 6. Add desired amount of salt, pepper, and grated Parmesan. Garnish with lemon wedges.

Notes
- Serve over rice or couscous.
- Boneless, skinless chicken thighs work too. They need a few extra minutes of browning and simmering.
- If the dish seems too dry, add chicken or vegetable broth or tomato juice or water by the tablespoonful till it reaches desired consistency.

Grief Is...

Grief is just one of those experiences
that people seldom truly *get*
unless they've felt its miserable sting.

Eleanor Haley

Dear sisters, expressing our grief as a metaphor can help us grasp it and communicate it. This excerpt by Donna Ashworth compares grief to a visitor and "love turned inside out."

Get used to grief my friend
for when it arrives
it won't be escorted out.

...So usher it in
let the grief win
it's love
turned inside out.

Some other metaphors for grief I have encountered are:

- Love with no place to go
- A gaunt gray wolf
- A heavy cloak
- A wrecking ball
- A knife in my heart

- An assassin or sniper
- A black hole
- A chronic condition
- A river of sadness
- A roller coaster in the dark
- A broken mirror
- An old fire dying out
- A Lazy Susan spinning
- A life sentence
- A lifeline connecting two people

"Analogies [and metaphors] are more useful than most people realize, especially when facing unfamiliar and confusing experiences because they help people communicate, understand, make connections, reason, and problem solve," writes Eleanor Haley.

In my own case, I recognize that the metaphors I expressed for my grief early on have changed, just as the emotional and physiological impact of grief changes over time. The metaphors you describe on the next page will likely change in the coming months and years.

- What are some of your metaphors for your specific grief? (What does your grief look like, feel like, remind you of?)
- Which of the metaphors above fit best how you feel right now?

At-home Fried Rice

No ordering, no credit card, no tip,
no trip to pick it up—so easy!

Ingredients	Directions
1 T. plus 1 tsp. peanut oil, divided (or other neutral oil)	1. Heat 1 T. oil in wok or medium skillet till glistening.
½ cup onion, chopped	2. Add onion, green pepper, celery, ginger, and fish sauce (if using) and stir fry on medium-high heat till softened (about 5 minutes).
¼ cup green bell pepper, chopped	
¼ cup celery, chopped	
1 T. fresh ginger, grated or finely chopped	
2 tsp. fish sauce (optional)	
1 egg, lightly beaten	3. In a separate small frying pan, heat 1 tsp. of oil. Add beaten egg and scramble, breaking into bite-sized pieces, and lightly salting and peppering.
1 cup cooked chicken or pork or ham, or shrimp, chopped	
1½ cups cooked rice	
Soy sauce (low sodium) to taste	
Toasted sesame seeds	4. To the vegetables add the egg, meat, and cooked rice. Gently toss all together with a spatula.

5. Continue lightly tossing to blend ingredients and cook until rice is hot and all ingredients are heated through.
6. Sprinkle soy sauce lightly over all. Garnish with sesame seeds.

Notes
- A perfect way to use left-over cooked rice or rotisserie chicken and really any vegetables.
- Omit the meat and fish sauce to make this a vegetarian dish.
- Rice cooked the day before seems to work best for this.

Feeling the Pain

The avoidance of grief
will only prolong the pain of grief.

David Kessler

*D*ear sisters, there is no right or wrong way to grieve our loss and there is no effective way around grief other than through it.

I worry about people who immediately move out of the house they shared with their mate or get rid of all their belongings as soon as possible because they can't bear the reminders. Grief can simply go underground, creating problems for the person later. This buried grief can invite use of dangerous substances or risky sex, or addictions, or risk-taking in general. Avoidance can create unexplained difficulty with relationships. So do let yourself feel your feelings.

There's a reason they call it "grief work." It is agonizing work and a grueling journey. Let the grief wash over you. Let the tears come. Accept the raw feelings for now without judgement.

Our instinct may be to escape the pain or to try to bury it. Our family pattern may be to ignore the need to grieve and to get on with things as if nothing happened. Some families stop talking about the person who died as if they never existed in trying to avoid the pain.

Some of us might try to intellectualize our pain instead of experiencing it. Searching the internet 24/7 for information or overanalyzing events can be a way to avoid the actual feelings.

The best long-term healing occurs if we can stay present to the pain and avoid judging ourselves. It will not continue this intensely forever. Our destination is peace with this new life, even though it is a life we didn't want or ask for.

If at any time you feel you may harm yourself, get immediate professional help. Start by calling 988 from anywhere in the U.S., any time of the day or night.

- What is the pattern in your family for grieving or expressing grief?
- How does your family celebrate a beloved person they have lost?
- How will you get help from a professional therapist or grief group if you need to deal with your present grief or buried grief from the past?

Pineapple Chicken (Sheet-Pan)

*Gorgeous colors—green, red, yellow—
all in one delectable dish.*

Ingredients	Directions
1 boneless, skinless chicken breast cut into 2-inch strips (8 oz.) ½ large green bell pepper cut into wide strips ⅓ cup red onion, cut into slices roughly the same size as the green pepper strips 1 cup fresh pineapple chunks 4 T. reduced-sodium soy sauce 2 tsp. honey 2 tsp. olive oil Roasted peanuts, chopped (dipping sauce ingredients on next page)	1. Preheat oven to 420° F. 2. Spray small baking sheet with nonstick cooking oil or line with parchment paper. 3. Combine chicken, bell pepper, onion, and pineapple in a medium bowl. 4. Add soy sauce , honey, and oil and toss. Marinate for 15 minutes. 5. Spread evenly on baking sheet and roast for 15-18 minutes or until chicken is cooked through (165°F) . 6. Drizzle lightly with teriyaki sauce and garnish with chopped peanuts if desired.

2 T. corn starch

¼ cup cold water

⅔ cup soy sauce

¾ cup orange juice

⅓ cup brown sugar

1 tsp. rice vinegar or apple cider vinegar

3 cloves garlic, minced

1 tsp. fresh ginger, minced

7. In a 2-cup glass measuring cup add cold water, then corn starch. Stir well so corn starch is fully dissolved.
8. Add remaining ingredients.
9. Microwave for 4-5 minutes. Mixture should be thick and bubbly.
10. Use as dipping sauce.

Notes

- Serve with brown rice or quinoa.
- Do not marinate chicken with pineapple for more than 15 minutes. (The chicken texture will deteriorate.)
- Be careful with this dish when opening the oven. The sheet pan will be very hot and steamy.
- Refrigerate leftover teriyaki sauce to use as a marinade or as a stir-fry sauce.

Feeling Nothing

Dear sisters, we cope with grief as best we can. Yet many people, following a death, have a feeling of nothingness. Medical science has a name for this feeling of total nothingness and emptiness: *anhedonia*.

The symptoms of anhedonia are commonly loss of interest in *everything* and it feels terrible. As grief writer Eleanor Haley says:

> It's hard to describe the feeling of nothingness to people who feel a general something-ness." [Anhedonia is] more like feeling empty, dead inside, emotionless, as though you have nothing to contribute, or as though you can't relate to the feelings and emotions of others (thus rendering social interaction problematic).

In this state, we may try to snap ourselves into feeling something by unhelpful strategies like alcohol or drugs or simply picking a fight with someone.

If we are numb and feel nothing, it doesn't mean we didn't love and care about the person we lost. It is how we are trying to survive that loss.

Haley advises that if this lack of feeling lasts longer than we are comfortable with or is negatively impacting daily life we should consider talking to a mental health professional. I didn't experience feelings of nothingness, but I am surely grateful I got expert professional support to help me move through the grief.

In the meantime, we who have been left behind need to treat ourselves with kindness, rest, get outside, take time to find or make healthy meals, ask for help, and, if possible, not do anything we don't feel able to do. We need time to grieve, each in our own way.

- In the past weeks, have you felt numb, invisible, empty, dead inside, emotionless, or unable to relate to others? Describe the feeling.
- What are three words or phrases that describe how you feel today?

Crisscross Baked Potato

This zesty spud will wake up your taste buds!

Ingredients	Directions
1 baking potato 1 T. olive oil 1 T. unsalted butter ½ tsp. kosher salt ½ tsp. dry mustard	1. Preheat oven to 350° F. 2. Scrub, dry, and then cut potato in half the long way. 3. With a paring knife, score the cut sides in a crisscross or cross-hatch fashion, about a quarter of an inch deep. 4. Melt butter with olive oil for a few seconds in the microwave and mix in salt and mustard. 5. Spread over cut sides of potato halves. 6. Bake for 50 minutes to an hour, depending on size and density of the potato.

Notes
- If using salted butter, use only ¼ tsp. salt.

More on Holidays

*D*ear sisters, given how challenging holidays are for grievers, they are getting another spot in this book.

I have tried very hard to reshape how I think about these landmark days that loom and threaten to bring up unbearable pain and anxiety. I try not to invest so much meaning in a particular day or week. It is a day (or several days) that will come and go.

I was alone for Christmas this past year. Yes, I did think about my husband and how we used to spend the holiday. But I let go of wanting things to be the same because they never will be. Instead, I thought of those past holidays with gratitude for what I had with him. I savored those memories without any expectations. It actually surprised me that the day passed just as any day might pass—morning to afternoon to evening.

Using New Year's Eve as an example, grief writer Eleanor Haley says, "Symbolically it can feel dramatic, significant, and weighted. But in reality, it's just another day. A single sleep. Nothing magical is changing or evaporating overnight tonight."

It is a single day (or week) out of a lifetime. This is one way to purposefully shape our own thinking, to take some of the emotional heat out of a holiday. At the same time, we can hold the hope of enjoying holidays in the future. See also "Holidays."

- What strategies have helped you cope with holidays so far?
- What days have been most difficult for you? What made them so hard?
- How can you plan ahead for the especially difficult anniversaries?

French Toast

A childhood favorite

Ingredients	Directions
1 egg ¼ cup whole milk ⅛ tsp. vanilla extract ⅛ tsp. sugar Pinch of cinnamon 2 slices of bread or Texas Toast 1 T. canola oil (or other neutral oil) Maple syrup or frozen raspberries, defrosted	1. Mix egg, milk, vanilla extract, sugar, and cinnamon in a shallow bowl or dish. 2. Dip both pieces of bread (both sides) in the egg mixture. 3. Heat a griddle or frying pan over medium heat. When hot, add oil to the pan. 4. When oil is hot, toast both sides of soaked bread until browned (2-3 minutes per side). 5. Top with syrup or raspberries.
Notes	

Stuck on the Sofa

*D*ear sisters, this happened to me. I had been sitting on the sofa in the darkened living room for over an hour. I felt like I was under water, the water pressure crushing my arms and legs, holding me down. I could not move off the sofa.

I had agreed to meet friends for dinner and a movie together. I HAD to get there. The world might come to an end, after all, if I didn't get to that restaurant!

I was already late. My anxiety was running wild. Yet something was still weighing me down—it was grief.

I did finally wrench myself off the sofa. I ran a cold washcloth over my face and stumbled out the door. (In the emotional shape I was in, I shouldn't have been driving.) I texted one of the friends but realized later that I had accidentally sent the text to a relative in a different state!

When I arrived half an hour late, I could feel that everyone was annoyed at having to wait. I felt miserable, but didn't offer an explanation, just apologized profusely.

Looking back, I can see that I had choices. I could have called with apologies that I didn't feel up to going out. I could have met the group at the theater. I could have told them what was happening to me, *but none of these options even occurred to me.*

My thinking was disordered that night. Grief overtakes us in strange and unexpected ways. We will be irrational at times. Our thinking may be clouded. We will need to alter plans sometimes. (Our friends will survive.) We may say things that are out of character. And when grief crushes us, we may be humiliated.

This is a time for showing compassion to ourselves. The expectations we held for ourselves before our loss become unrealistic and possibly unattainable in grief. We need to hold ourselves gently as we would a friend or loved one suffering unbearable pain. And resist being ashamed of grief and its manifestations, as these spring from love for the partner we have lost.

- What behaviors have you noticed since the death that are not typical for you?
- What expectations do you have for yourself that might not be realistic as you try to survive your loss?

Oven-Fried Sweet Potato

Simplest recipe in this book!

Ingredients	Directions
1 large sweet potato 2 tsp. olive oil Salt to taste	1. Preheat oven to 450° F. 2. Wash and peel sweet potato and cut into ¾ inch disks. 3. Place the oil on a small baking sheet and one by one, roll the slices in the oil. (They need only a light coating.) 4. Avoid crowding them—the slices need air to get crispy. 5. Bake in preheated oven for 15 minutes, turn them and lower heat to 425° F. and cook 5-10 minutes longer. 6. Sprinkle lightly with salt before serving.

Notes
- To make peeling easier, cut off both ends first and peel the skin off in strips.
- To make cleanup easier, place a sheet of parchment on the baking pan. Spread the oil onto the parchment paper with a spoon before adding the sweet potato slices.
- Avoid using glass baking dishes for this recipe as the high heat could cause breakage.

Gratitude

When you arise in the morning,
think of what a precious privilege it is to be alive
—to breathe, to think, to enjoy, to love.

Marcus Aurelius

*D*ear sisters, in the depth of grief, we may not feel grateful for anything. At least part of this is due to biology. Our brains are wired to remember and pay more attention to the negative than to the positive. This is considered a survival mechanism to ensure humans remember what's dangerous. Psychologist Rick Hanson describes our minds as Velcro for the bad experiences (everything sticks) and Teflon for the good (nothing sticks).

When I was at a low point, I began following meditation teacher Andy Puddicombe. At Andy's suggestion, I now take thirty seconds before even getting out of bed in the morning to sit up and be grateful I woke up. It's really a perfect way to start the day.

In my almost nightly letters to Matt, I often list the things I am grateful for. To be clear, gratitude doesn't take away the longing. But taking stock of what we are grateful for is a great answer to feeling hopeless. Naming what we appreciate helps us recognize that our lives hold more than grief and loss. Writing these things helps them stick in our awareness, perhaps like Velcro.

- List what about your life you are grateful for (people, places, things, feelings). Be specific. For example, "My sister who checks on me every other day."
- On your list, what are the three things you are *most* grateful for? Put a star by those.

Caramelized Brussels Sprouts

*These little jewels can be tame or
as hot-peppery as you like.*

Ingredients	Directions
8 oz. fresh Brussels sprouts 2 garlic cloves, sliced thin 1 heaping T. Parmesan cheese, grated 1 T. lemon juice Salt and pepper to taste 3 T. extra virgin olive oil Fresh lemon wedges for serving	1. Line a cookie sheet or baking dish with parchment paper or foil. 2. Preheat oven to 400° F. 3. Rinse Brussels sprouts, removing loose outer leaves and hard stems. Dry thoroughly in a towel or lettuce spinner. 4. Cut sprouts in half. Smaller ones can be left whole. In smaller ones, cut an X in the stem end to help them cook evenly. 5. Place sprouts cut side down in the baking dish or cookie sheet.

6. Add the garlic slices, Parmesan cheese, lemon juice, and salt and pepper.
7. Drizzle olive oil over all. Mix well so sprouts are coated. (Rearrange as needed to keep the sprouts cut-side down. Avoid over- crowding.)
8. Roast in the preheated oven uncovered about 20-30 minutes until crispy, brown, and caramelized on the outside and tender on the inside.
9. Serve with lemon wedges.

Notes
- High heat and fast cooking reduces bitterness in Brussels sprouts.
- If your oven overheats and burns things, you can add the garlic and the Parmesan in the last half of the cooking time. Drizzle olive oil on the garlic and Parm mixture before scattering it over the hot sprouts.
- For extra heat, add a dusting of red pepper flakes prior to roasting.

Weird About Grief

*D*ear sisters, our culture is weird about grief and death. In past centuries, it was clear when someone had died. A black wreath on the door was an unmistakable sign that death had visited. Grieving people wore black clothing for six months to a year. Mourning was public.

Not anymore. No one can tell we are in mourning and weighed down with grief unless we tell them.

People in the past prepared the body themselves with loved ones lying in state in the living room. It may seem macabre to us now, but it normalized death as part of life. Today, death and grief are mostly taboo discussion topics.

On average in the U.S., three days off are allotted for the death of a lifetime companion. The prevailing assumption is that, after a couple of days at most, people should be ready to get back to work and be productive as usual.

Grief in the U.S. is treated as a personal problem. This view is not shared with much of the world where joyful ceremonies, dances, feasts, multi-day observances, events with hundreds of people, and many opportunities exist to mourn as a community. In the Western world, people often don't say anything because they don't know what to say. People may even avoid a bereaved person for fear of saying the wrong thing.

Judaism offers an exception, maintaining traditions to help people grieve together. During Shiva—a period of time after a death, traditionally seven days—people come to the mourners' home to support them. People bring food and remain to sit and talk with and comfort the family.

We may feel alone in our grief. We will likely be expected to get over it, carry on, stiff upper lip and all that. We may get messages from others that we are grieving too much, not enough, or too long. Others may suggest, subtly or not, that tears signal weakness. But grief has no timeline and every person experiences it in their own way.

Yet we can be our own best advocate. Ask for what we need, connect with supportive people, talk to the boss, get help, accept all our feelings, reach out to other grievers, set boundaries, let the tears flow, be extra kind to ourselves and most of all, we will avoid anyone who says we should get over it. We will heal in our own time.

- What support from others are you receiving as you grieve?
- What else might you need right now from family, workplace, religious institution, or community?
- How can you ask for the support you need? Where and when will you start?

Turkey Meatloaf

*For the main course on Sunday
and sandwiches on Monday!*

Ingredients	Directions
¾ lbs. ground turkey 6 T. dry breadcrumbs or panko ¼ cup milk ½ cup onions, chopped 1 small egg, beaten ¾ tsp. kosher salt ⅛ tsp. ground black pepper 1 small clove garlic, minced Cooking spray or vegetable oil for greasing baking pan ¼ cup ketchup 2 T. brown sugar 1 T. red wine vinegar (or use store-bought barbeque sauce for the topping)	1. Preheat oven to 350° F. 2. With cooking spray or vegetable oil, lightly grease loaf pan, 8 x 8 baking dish, or cookie sheet that has edges. (Or line with parchment paper.) 3. Using a fork, mix turkey, crumbs, milk, onion, egg, salt, pepper and garlic in a bowl. 4. For topping, in a separate small bowl, mix ketchup, brown sugar, and wine vinegar. Set aside. 5. Form a loaf with turkey mixture and place on prepared baking pan or dish. 6. Bake in preheated oven for 30 minutes.

7. Remove loaf pan from oven and drain or spoon out any accumulated juices. Spread topping over it and return to oven.

8. Bake loaf about another 25-30 minutes. A meat thermometer should read 165° F.

Notes

- You can also cut into loaf to ensure that it is no longer pink in the center.
- I use 97%-lean ground turkey for the added flavor.
- This meatloaf freezes well.

Grieving the Present

*D*ear sisters, we grieve for ourselves and our situation. Our normal life has changed when other people's normal lives have not. We wonder sometimes how everyone can just go on with their lives as if nothing has happened.

We grieve because we are scared stiff, scared of being alone forever, scared of not knowing what to do, scared of making big mistakes, scared about finances, scared about so many things.

We grieve having to make every single decision by ourselves.

We grieve the friends who used to be ours but somehow have drifted away now that it's just "me" and not "we."

We grieve walking alone. While visiting Paris shortly after Matt died, for example, I saw an elderly couple coming out of the Metro holding hands. They radiated an aura of contentment. That sight was so emotionally charged for me that I got dizzy and fell flat on my face on the Parisien sidewalk!

David Kessler says that a conscious decision is required in order to live our lives fully again.

> But when you're ready to hope again, you will be able to find it. Bad days don't have to be your eternal destiny. That doesn't mean your grief will get smaller over time. It means you must get bigger.
>
> …You can keep growing and finding ways to live a good and someday even a joyous life, one enriched by the lessons and love of the person who died.

Once we have survived the early days of loss, we can make a commitment to ourselves and even to the lover we have lost that we will live again. Not just survive, but live fully the life we have been given.

- At this place in your grief journey, what do you find the most difficult?
- What are your hopes for your future healing?

....

....

....

....

....

....

....

....

....

....

....

....

....

Carrot Cake

A favorite way to eat your vegetables!

Ingredients	Directions
¼ cup sugar 2 T. butter, melted 1 large egg yolk ⅛ tsp. vanilla extract ¼ cup all-purpose flour ¼ tsp. baking powder ⅛ tsp. cinnamon ⅛ tsp. salt 1 T. milk (skim) ¼ cup carrots, finely grated 1 T. pecans, chopped 1 oz. cream cheese, softened 1 T. butter, softened (not melted) ¼ cup powdered sugar ¼ tsp. vanilla extract	1. Preheat oven to 350° F. Lightly butter a 10-oz. ramekin. 2. In a small bowl, mix sugar, melted butter, egg yolk, and vanilla with an electric hand mixer on medium speed until well-mixed, about 45 seconds. 3. Add the dry ingredients and mix with a hand mixer on medium speed until combined. 4. Add milk and mix well. 5. Fold in grated carrots and pecans and pour into ramekin.

6. Bake for 20-23 minutes or until a toothpick inserted in the center comes out clean. Be careful not to overbake.

7. For the frosting, combine cream cheese and soft butter in a small bowl. Stir with a spoon until smooth.

8. Add powdered sugar and vanilla and mix until smooth.

9. Spread over top of cooled cake.

Notes

- Chopped walnuts may be used in place of pecans.
- Neutral vegetable oil may be used in place of melted butter.

Getting Things Done

Dear sisters, our grief is so heavy. Especially in early grief, it can be overwhelming to take a shower or pay a credit card bill.

One thing that helped me is what I call "cueing-things-up-for-success"—and believe me, my "success" at first was pretty modest, such as putting in a load of laundry or making a phone call. Instead of doing each task all at once, I got out the things I would need to do the "thing" the next morning or later in the day. Some examples:

- For a shower, it was setting out towels and supplies for hair-washing.
- For paying a bill, it was taking the bill out of the envelope and making it ready to pay. (Even addressing the envelope if it was something to mail).
- For making real food, it was setting out the cutting board and knife and bowls.
- For changing sheets, it was putting out the fresh sheets on the nightstand.
- For making a call, it was having the number on a sticky note with a time I planned to make the call.

Neuroscientist Lynda Shaw says that the brain responds positively to "bite-sized goals." This explains why it can be satisfying to check off things on a daily To-Do list.

This has helped me to break tasks into smaller steps and create the visual cues, like towels and bowls and stamps set out where I can see them. If I don't have to do the whole thing at once, I find it's less challenging.

I still use this method to get some things done.

- What tasks are most challenging for you these days?
- How could you break the hardest tasks into smaller steps?
- What visual reminders or friends could help you get each task started?

Pasta e Fagioli Soup

A hearty, packed-with-flavor soup,
like in a popular Italian restaurant!

Ingredients	Directions
⅓ cup uncooked ditalini or elbow pasta 1 T. olive oil, divided 1 or 2 spicy or mild Italian sausages, casing removed (or 4-8 oz uncooked bulk Italian sausage) 1 clove garlic, minced ⅓ c. onion, diced 1 small rib celery, diced 1 small carrot, peeled and diced 1 cup chicken broth ½ cup water 1-14.5 oz. can diced tomatoes 1 T. tomato paste mixed with 1 T. water ½ tsp. dried basil ¼ tsp. dried oregano ¼ tsp. dried thyme Half a 15.5 oz. can of kidney beans, drained Kosher salt and black pepper	1. Cook pasta in a large pot of boiling water according to package directions, but just a little underdone—*al dente.* Drain and set aside. 2. Heat 1/2 T. olive oil in a soup pot. Add Italian sausage and cook until browned, about 2-3 minutes. Crumble as it cooks and drain off excess fat. Set aside. 3. Add remaining 1/2 T. olive oil to pot. Stir in garlic, onion, carrots, and celery. Stir-fry until tender, about 3 minutes.

4. Whisk in chicken broth, diced tomatoes, tomato paste mixture, basil, oregano, thyme, Italian sausage, and water. Season with salt and pepper to taste.

5. Bring to a boil then reduce heat and simmer, covered until vegetables are tender, about 10 minutes.

6. Stir in beans and pasta until heated through.

Notes

- Tomato paste in a tube is handy for cooking smaller batches.
- Use remaining canned kidney beans in salads.
- If you soak and cook beans from scratch, use ⅓ cup of dry beans.

You Cost Me

*D*ear sisters, I learned something very valuable from my friend who lived in Bolivia. She was exasperated. "Oh, that woman," she said in Spanish, "*me cuesta*—she costs me!"

Spending time with a different friend, she might say the opposite, "That friend—*me llena*—fills me!"

I now find myself thinking in terms of people and experiences that either *cost me* or *fill me*.

The friend who *costs you* might tell you that you shouldn't feel a certain way or judge your decisions. The friend who *costs you* may tempt you to censor yourself to avoid criticism. A friend who *costs you* doesn't build you up but rather makes you feel unsure of yourself. Another *me cuesta* manifestation is people who are so excessively needy themselves that they drain the life out of you.

The friend who *fills you* comforts you just by being there. One who *fills you* notices your likes and dislikes and is genuinely interested in what is happening in your life. A friend who *fills you* supports you as you heal and adjust to new life circumstances.

In ordinary circumstances, I would suggest addressing a friend's upsetting behaviors more directly. For example, "Would you call me, please, before you come over? I want to be sure I'm dressed." Grief and mourning, however, are not ordinary circumstances and we may not have the bandwidth to be perfectly direct.

To avoid spending time with friends who cost us, we can say is something like: "I am not up to it right now, but thank you."

If they argue or try to cajole us into doing something we don't want to do, we can simply repeat, "I am not up to it right now, but thank you."

We are grieving. We do not owe anyone further explanation, but we can surely change the subject: "Have you started planting your flowers yet?"

To survive the pain we are in, we need all our energy just to get through these days—we don't have extra to waste on people or activities that "cost us."

- Who are your *me llena* friends or family members who lift your spirits and support you?
- What, specifically, do they do that you appreciate?

Cherry Chicken Salad

The sweet-tart cherries make this chicken salad sing.

Ingredients	Directions
1 cup cooked chicken, cubed, bite-sized	1. Mix chicken, cherries, green onion, and celery in a medium bowl.
¼ cup dried pitted tart cherries	
1 green onion, thinly sliced (white and green parts)	2. In a small bowl, mix mayonnaise, yogurt, lemon juice, salt and pepper until blended.
1 T. celery, chopped	
2 T. mayonnaise	3. Stir into chicken mixture.
1 T. plain yogurt	
2 tsp. fresh lemon juice	4. Cover and refrigerate for an hour before serving.
Salt to taste	
Freshly ground black pepper to taste	

Notes
- Serve over lettuce or in a sandwich.
- Red or green seedless grapes go nicely alongside.

Special Days

Death ends a life, not a relationship.

Author unknown

Their birthday? Your anniversary? Their death anniversary? Dear sisters, those will not be ordinary days for us. If working or volunteering, consider taking the day off if that sounds good to you. Here are some options for remembering and celebrating them.

- Cook or buy their favorite meal.
- Wear something they gave you—jewelry, clothing, gloves.
- Walk in a place you enjoyed together.
- Have a picnic in a place you enjoyed together.
- Find photos of the two of you together.
- Call a friend or family member to share a memory.
- Light a candle in their memory.
- Make a special ornament or decoration in their honor.
- Donate flowers at your place of worship in memory.
- Look through photo albums.
- Watch old family videos.
- Watch a movie they loved.
- Ask others to tell stories about the person or share favorite memories.
- Learn more about their family tree and ancestors to share with the family.

- Make a playlist of songs they enjoyed.
- Call one of their close friends.
- What else?

A dear friend told me she had dreaded the date on the calendar that would mark a year after her husband's death. Just looking at the calendar and thinking of the date approaching caused her great upset. How would she possibly get through it? When the day came, it wasn't anything as frightful as she had imagined. She thought about her husband with love and cried some tears, but the day was so much easier than the fear she had held for weeks before.

- What days do you celebrate in remembrance of your beloved?
- How do you make each of them a special day?
- What other commemorative activities might you try? Will you?

Beef Stroganoff Meatloaf

Definitely not the same-old-meatloaf recipe.

Ingredients	Directions
8 oz. ground beef (chuck) 1 T. panko crumbs ¼ cup onions, finely chopped ½ beaten egg ⅓ cup canned mushrooms, drained and chopped (half of a 4-oz. can) 1 tsp. Worcestershire sauce 1½ T. plain Greek yogurt 1 T. dry red wine ½ tp. coarsely ground black pepper ¼ tsp. kosher salt (sauce ingredients on next page.)	1. Preheat oven to 350° F. 2. Combine all meatloaf ingredients in a medium bowl and mix well with a fork. 3. Shape into a loaf, place in a loaf baking dish or on a rack in a roasting pan lined with parchment paper. 4. Bake for 50-55 minutes or until meat thermometer reads 170°F. Remove and keep warm.

1 tsp. beef bouillon
granules or ½ tsp. beef
soup base

2 tsp. all-purpose flour

¼ cup hot water

⅔ cup sour cream

2 T. green onions, sliced
fine

⅛ tsp. ground white
pepper

Chopped fresh parsley

5. For sauce, combine
bouillon granules or
soup base, flour and
water in a frying pan.
Whisk together well.
(The flour should
have no raw taste
when done.)

6. Cook over medium
heat till thickened
(2-5 minutes).

7. Combine sour cream,
green onions, and
white pepper.

8. Add sour cream
mixture slowly to
bouillon mixture,
stirring well.

9. Cook over low heat
till heated through,
stirring constantly.
(*Do not boil.*)

10. Spoon sauce over
meatloaf and serve
with mashed potatoes
or noodles or rice.

11. Garnish with parsley.

Notes

- To end up with half an egg, break egg into small bowl, whisk with a fork and then simple use only half of it.
- If using fresh chopped mushrooms for meatloaf, sauté in 2 tsp. neutral oil before adding to meat mixture.

The Great Healer

In every walk with nature,
one receives far more than he seeks.

John Muir

*D*ear sisters, Mother Nature is the great healer. That is what the doctor said to me in discussing my depression following Matt's death. He said, you have to get outside in nature for the sake of your body and your mind and your spirit.

I knew that was probably true. I always felt better after taking a walk outside. But I wondered, what is it about Mother Nature that can help us heal on our grief journey?

We are part of nature, something easy to forget in our hi-tech lives. Being outside in nature directly benefits us physically. Numerous studies around the world show that when people are outside in nature, positive neurochemical changes take place in our brains and our blood pressure goes down. Sunlight stimulates Vitamin D absorption and increases calcium levels, benefiting the immune system.

Grievers can easily get caught in cycles of obsessive thoughts of guilt and regret. These obsessive thought cycles prevent us from living in the present and enjoying the life we do have. Being with nature helps us to focus on the here and now—that baby rabbit that hopped out on the path, the fragrance of the pines, the squawk of a Blue Jay warning us away from the nest.

Mother Nature beguiles all our senses—seeing, hearing, smelling, feeling, even tasting if we run into some wild blueberries. To get the most benefit, we are advised to leave our headphones at home and listen just to the outdoors.

Have you heard of "Forest Bathing?" It has nothing to do with soap and water. The concept, coined in Japan, but enjoyed by humans over millennia is simply being in the forest and soaking it all in. There is no destination or goal, other than to notice and appreciate. In studying the positive physical and emotional effects of Forest Bathing, researchers have discovered that evergreen tree bark gives off essential oils that when breathed in, boost the immune system.

Gardening can be uniquely healing. Every little plant is a miracle. Getting close to the earth, planting the seeds, caring for the plants, and then enjoying the harvest. We experience first-hand the cycle of all life—birth through death—and we see that change is the only constant in the natural world. Planting a Memorial Garden could be the perfect way to honor a dear partner and get the air and sunshine we need.

So try to get outside every day, even just for a walk around the block, or a few moments on the porch breathing in the fresh air, or a walk in the woods or on the beach. Look up at the birds of the air and marvel.

- In what ways do you connect with nature now?
- How do you feel when you do? Why?
- With what else can you interact regularly in nature to find comfort and healing? Name at least three specific things or places.

Turkey-Broccoli Bake

*A rich rendez-vous of flavors that
happens to be keto-friendly.*

Ingredients	Directions
1 T. canola oil ½ cup celery, diced (1-2 ribs) ¼ cup onion, diced ¼ cup green pepper (diced) 1 clove garlic, minced ½ cup fresh mushrooms, sliced 1 cup fresh broccoli, chopped ½ tsp. of your favorite seasoning blend (or ¼ tsp. dried thyme) ⅛ tsp. kosher salt (optional) ¼ tsp. ground pepper 1 T. dry white wine or hot water or broth 4 oz. cream cheese, cut into 16 cubes 3/4 cup cooked turkey (or chicken), cubed	1. Preheat oven to 350° F. 2. Heat oil in a large frying pan over medium heat and cook vegetables and garlic (about 5 minutes). You want some good crunch left in the veggies. 3. Push veggies to the side and fry mushrooms in the middle of the pan, stirring occasionally till they start to brown. 4. Add the seasoning blend (or thyme), salt, and pepper, and wine or hot water or broth. Mix gently.

5. Add the cubed cream cheese to the pan, reduce heat to low and cook for several minutes until the cream cheese is melted, stirring frequently.
6. Add cooked turkey or chicken. Mix gently. (If the mixture looks too dry, add another tablespoon of wine or hot water or broth.)
7. Pour mixture into a buttered casserole dish and bake uncovered until golden (10-15 minutes).

Notes

- If making this with chicken, use cooked boneless, skinless chicken thighs.

Homesick

*D*ear sisters, when Matt first died, the pain was a knife stuck in my heart and dragged through my body. Now the pain is an ache in my bones that I am getting used to. I often feel homesick.

It helps to know that it's normal to feel homesick, to miss the life we had before death changed so much. Here are some strategies for addressing homesickness.

1. Get out of the house. If we stay in bed all day or on the sofa watching TV, we will end up bored and eventually ill, all of which makes homesickness worse. Go to a coffee shop, pick up some groceries, check out the library, take yourself to a movie or invite a friend.

2. Walk outside. As you know, Mother Nature is the great healer. We will almost always feel better after a walk outside even if the weather isn't great. Just bundle up.

3. Meet new people—people who didn't know the person you have lost can help you adjust to your new life. It takes energy to extend yourself to new acquaintances, but you get back energy too. I took a French class three months after Matt died. It was oddly refreshing to walk into a room full of people who didn't know my story.

4. Make a schedule for yourself. You probably won't be able to do this early in your grief journey, but as soon as you can figure out what is important for you to do every day,

no matter what, make a schedule and do your best to keep it. (Perfection not required.) Having a schedule provides a measure of control for you.

5. Make a bullet journal or "BuJo." This is a popular paper-based system for journaling and recording your schedule. Some people's bullet journals are works of art. Mine is just a small notebook with a page for each day. Before I retired as a consultant, I used an online calendar. In my life now, it is much easier to use my paper bullet journal. (And it's fun to decorate the pages with stencils, different pen colors, washi tape, and stickers if that is your thing.)

6. Connect with other people. Invite a friend to come over for coffee or tea. Or call or text family members who are also affected by the loss. Chances are, they would welcome the TLC.

7. Get away from home for a short trip or outing. This may seem counter-intuitive when we are already feeling homesick, but a novel experience will create new memories and engage us with interesting sights and sounds. We will always learn something new.

8. Do something nice for yourself every day. You will define "something nice" in your own way. Make a space in your calendar or bullet journal to plan what nice thing you will do for yourself each day.

- How do you respond to the feeling of homesickness?
- Which of the actions suggested above do you already do?
- Which one(s) will you try out? How and when?

Green Velvet Cashew Sauce

This creamy green sauce is flecked with fresh herbs.
Great on poached salmon or salmon cakes!

Ingredients	Directions
¼ cup raw, unsalted cashews ¼ cup milk (whole or 2%) ¼ cup flat-leaf parsley, chopped 3 T. fresh dill, chopped 1 T. fresh mint, chopped 2 T. mayonnaise 1 T. fresh lemon juice ⅛ tsp. sea salt (or more to taste) ⅛ tsp. black pepper	1. Place raw cashews in a small bowl. Cover with cool water and refrigerate at least 4 hour, even overnight. 2. Drain and rinse soaked cashews. 3. Add cashews and remaining ingredients to a food processor or high-speed blender. Blend well, till smooth. 4. Cover and refrigerate for up two days.

Notes

- To make this vegan, for serving over rice or grains, use ¼ cup of plain, unsweetened almond milk and 2 T. vegan mayonnaise.

Anger

*A*ngry? Grievers are often white-hot angry. Anger, as you probably know, is one of the common stages of grief identified by Elizabeth Kübler-Ross (along with Denial, Bargaining, Depression, and Acceptance). Even Kübler-Ross said these stages don't happen in a nice, neat sequence, that they are more accurately dimensions of grief. One moves in and out of them, hopefully moving toward acceptance and finding renewed meaning in our own life.

Who or what are you angry at? The beloved mate who abandoned you by dying? The doctors who didn't save him? Family members who made it all harder? Friends who didn't show up? You for not understanding what was happening? God? Fate?

Many of us have been taught that anger is a bad thing, a sin even. Yet anger is an emotion that signals something is wrong. Anger is a manifestation of our grief: We feel it because we loved what has been lost.

Anger does not take well to being denied or pushed down. It easily morphs into depression or illness or it comes out sideways as a harsh comment or barked demand or harmful behaviors.

Anger can also serve as a way to avoid the unspeakable pain. Even if a bereaved person feels mostly enraged, the sadness is still underneath the fury. If we can't acknowledge both the anger and the sadness, we are delayed in moving forward with recreating our lives.

When anger becomes the long-term response, little room is left for healing, joy, curiosity, compassion, love, and other good things. Long-term anger will produce physical problems.

It is also true that anger expressed can energize us and lead to positive action. Think of the families who have lost loved ones to illness or violence or overdoses who have created action and advocacy groups or research foundations for treatment and prevention. Volunteering with these groups or donating to them is something many of us can do.

It's worthwhile to explore and express our own anger—to give it voice and listen to the pain that vibrates underneath it. Writing about it, creating art or music, pounding a pillow, yelling where you can't be heard, talking to others, working with a grief group or therapist—these are all strategies for dealing up front with anger following death. Some people even give their anger a name and greet it when it shows up.

Give voice to anger, not to stew in it or be held hostage by it. Rather to let it move on so we can feel the sadness and work toward rebuilding our own life.

- I am angry about my beloved's death because…
- I tend to express this anger by…
- If my anger had a name, it would be…

Pineapple Upside Down Cake

Decadent, with a sticky-sweet pineapple crown.

Ingredients	Directions
1 T. melted butter 1 T. brown sugar 1 pineapple ring (canned or fresh) 1 maraschino cherry 1 T. butter, very soft 3 T. sugar 1 egg yolk ⅛ tsp. vanilla extract 3 T. flour ⅛ tsp. baking powder ⅛ tsp. salt 1 T. milk (whole or skim)	1. Preheat oven to 350° F. Butter sides of a small ramekin (10 oz.). 2. Mix melted butter and brown sugar together in a small bowl. Pour into ramekin and spread with a spoon so the entire bottom of the ramekin is covered. 3. Top with pineapple ring and add the cherry in the center hole. 4. In a small bowl, mix together softened butter and sugar until well-combined. 5. Add egg yolk and vanilla extract and mix well.

6. Add flour, baking powder, and salt and stir until just combined.
7. Stir in milk.
8. Pour batter into the ramekin and use the back of a spoon to smooth the batter over the pineapple.
9. Bake for 30 minutes or until toothpick inserted into the center comes out clean.
10. Cool on rack for 15 minutes. Place a plate over the top of the ramekin and invert. The cake should come out easily onto the plate.

Notes
- You can use 3 oz. of sliced apples, pineapple chunks, or sliced peaches or pears in place of the pineapple ring and cherry.

The Privilege of Grief

Dear sisters, after 9/11/01, Queen Elizabeth II of Great Britain stated that grief is the price we pay for love. If we are grieving, we have experienced love, the greatest gift a human can receive. A poem written by my friend, Nancy Cross Dunham, imagines grief as a friend. Her poem was featured on National Public Radio.

what I'm learning about grief ...

what I'm learning about grief ...
is that it need not be
a heavy gray shawl
to wrap myself in,
clutching my arms tightly
across my chest
nor ...
need it be
a granite rock
that I should try
to push away
neither is it ...
... at least, no longer ...
a vast dark ocean
ready to pick me up
and slap me down
without warning

what I'm learning about grief ...
is that it is not me,
but that it offers
to become a friend
a friend ...
who will lightly lay a hand
on my shoulder
when tears come in the dark
a friend ...
who will laugh
out loud with me
at remembered silly moments
a friend ...
who can still hear
the music of our life
what I'm learning about grief ...
is that this friend
doesn't intend
to leave me
but promises
to hold my hand
to carry my memories
a friend ...
who will bear witness to my love
as I venture
toward the next day
and the following night

Poet Donna Ashworth says it this way: "Remember. Grief came to you my friend because love came first."

- Do you relate to the poem on the previous pages? What words or phrases stand out?
- When you think of your own grief, what other words or phrases come into your mind?
- Use your words and phrases to create a short poem about grief. Share it with a friend (or in prayer).

Twice-baked Potato

It's much better than half-baked!

Ingredients	Directions
1 large russet potato 1 T. onion, chopped fine 1 T. green bell pepper, chopped fine 1 T. carrot, grated fine 2-3 T. milk 1 tsp. butter (optional) 1 T. sour cream ¼ tsp. salt ⅛ tsp. pepper 2 T. Parmesan cheese, grated finely 3 T. cheddar, grated Olive oil or other neutral oil Sunflower seeds (optional)	1. Scrub potato and oil the skin with olive oil. 2. Place potato on oven rack in 350° F. oven. Bake 50-75 minutes. (See Notes.) 3. Heat 2 tsp. olive oil in a small frying pan. Sauté onion, green pepper, and carrot on medium heat till tender-crisp (5-10 minutes). 4. Remove potato from oven and allow to cool until you can handle it comfortably. Slice in half the long way and scoop out the innards. Place in a medium bowl. 5. Mash well with a potato masher.

6. Heat milk and butter, if using, in microwave 20-30 seconds and blend into potatoes.

7. Blend in sour cream, green pepper mixture, salt and pepper. Consistency should be like fluffy mashed potatoes—not dry, not wet.

8. Spoon the potato mixture back into the potato skins. Sprinkle with sunflower seeds if using.

9. Sprinkle Parmesan cheese, then cheddar over potato halves.

10. Bake in 400° F. oven for 10 minutes or till cheese is melted.

Notes

- Place a baking sheet under oven rack in Step 2 to catch oil from the potato.
- In Step 2, potato is done when it is soft enough to pierce through with a fork.
- Amounts are approximate due to variation in size of potatoes.

Photographs

*D*ear sisters, you might remember this too. When I was a girl, we had to send our camera film somewhere to be developed and it took two weeks and was very expensive. I remember how incredulous I was when 24-hour photo developing was introduced.

Because photographs were so costly and you had to wait so long to get them, a person kept all the photos, discarding only the most ruined ones. (At least I did.) The result is multiple boxes of old photos, some in albums, most not.

Now in the age of smart phones, we don't have a lot of photos to hold in our hands or put in a frame. They are in our phones or on our hard drives. Quite the opposite of the past.

Photographs of the much-loved partner who died are comforting to some but bring up unbearable sadness for others. I have pictures of Matt in various rooms around the house.

Savoring photographs and remembering happy times together can balance out more painful thoughts and emotions. For me, having a few hard copy photos to look at and hold in my hands is more comforting than looking at them on my phone screen. Here are some ideas.

- Look on your phone for a few especially meaningful photos and send them directly to a drug store or service center to be made into prints.

- Collect 5-10 photos from happy times and place in a small, inexpensive mini-photo album to keep near you and even take with you when you travel.
- Have special photos made into metal pictures that stand on their own and look great.
- Look through the prints you have. Decide on the ones you want to keep. Divide up the rest of the photos to give to family members and friends. Throw away duplicates or botched pictures. (Decluttering can be very therapeutic.)
- Create a montage of treasured photos to hang on a wall.
- What else?

- In looking through your photos of your beloved, which ones are the most precious to you? What, specifically, makes each one so special?
- What other comforting ideas might you have for using your photographs?

Lemon Shrimp Pasta

A Mediterranean diet treasure and everything is cooked in one big pot.

Ingredients	Directions
3 oz. linguini 2 tsp. olive oil 2 T. butter, divided 1½ cloves garlic, minced ½ tsp. chili powder ½ tsp. red pepper flakes 8 ounces large uncooked, deveined shrimp (About 17 shrimp) Salt and pepper to taste ½ tsp. Italian seasoning 2 cups packed fresh baby spinach ¼ cup Parmesan cheese, shredded 2 tsp. fresh parsley, chopped 1-2 tsp. lemon juice ½ cup saved pasta cooking water (if needed)	1. Cook pasta in a large pot according to package directions. Drain (remembering to save half a cup of cooking water) and set aside. 2. In the same pan, heat olive oil and 1 T. of butter. Add garlic, chili powder, and red pepper and cook until fragrant (about 1 minute). 3. Add the shrimp and salt and pepper and cook until shrimp start to turn pink. 4. Add Italian seasoning and spinach and cook until spinach is wilted.

5. Add pasta back to the pot along with remaining 1 T. butter, Parmesan, and parsley. Stir until butter is melted.

6. Add lemon juice just before serving. If the dish seems too thick, add some reheated pasta cooking water one tablespoon at a time till it reaches the desired consistency.

7. Serve hot.

Notes

- If your shrimp is not shelled, you will need a 12 oz. package.
- Set out a measuring cup next to the pasta pot as it cooks as a reminder to save some of the cooking water. It's easy to forget until it's too late. I've sure done that.

Scattered

Dear sisters, someone dear to me is neurodivergent which means her brain functions differently than other brains might. Over the years, this has given her challenges with focus and attention. Being neurodivergent has also gifted her with amazing intelligence along with artistic, linguistic, and creative abilities. She recently shared with me the analogy of the June Bug.

I had mentioned to her that, in my grief, I alternated between being unable to do anything at all and trying to do about a hundred things at once. Starting the dishes, stopping to water the plants, stepping out to bring in the mail, checking my bank balance on-line, all within the same few minutes. Not only did this pattern deplete my energy; this random activity meant that I never finished much of anything. I was scattered.

She suggested that I consider the June Bug hanging onto the screen door. Once in place, on the screen, the June Bug does not move. It is determined to reach the chosen light source. I don't know what the June Bug thinks about while attached to a screen, but I know it doesn't think about doing other things. That is one focused bug.

So when I catch myself in my "scattered" pattern, I just chirp out loud, "June Bug." This stops me in my tracks and reminds me to finish what I am doing before I fixate on something else.

We cannot expect ourselves to do all the things we did before grief took us out at the knees. But if there is something we ourselves really want to get done and are feeling scattered, perhaps "June Bug" is just the right thing to say, whisper, or even sing!

- What do you think of the June Bug analogy?
- Do you ever find yourself in a "scattered" pattern because of your grief? Describe what happens.

Chili

Make this when chili sounds wonderful but a huge vat of it is out of the question.

Ingredients	Directions
2 tsp. canola or olive oil 1 small onion, chopped fine (⅓ cup) ¼ cup green pepper, coarsely chopped ¼ cup celery, coarsely chopped 1 large garlic clove, minced 1 T. chili powder (or to taste) ¼ tsp. ground cumin ¼ tsp. red pepper flakes or cayenne pepper 8 oz. ground beef (chuck) or ground turkey 1 can (14.5 oz.) tomatoes (whole, petite diced, or crushed) 1 cup beef broth ¾ cup canned kidney or pinto beans, rinsed and drained	1. Heat oil in medium saucepan over medium heat till shimmering. 2. Add onion, green pepper, celery, garlic, chili powder, cumin, and pepper flakes or cayenne. 3. Cook, stirring often, until vegetables soften, 3-5 minutes. Add ground beef or turkey, breaking it up with a turner or spoon, just until no longer pink (3-5 minutes). 4. Stir in tomatoes and their juice and beef broth. Break up tomatoes with turner or spoon. Heat to a simmer.

Garnishes

Grated cheese, cooked and crumbled bacon, sour cream, plain yogurt, sliced green onions, chips, or cilantro.

5. Cover, reduce heat to medium low and simmer for 45 minutes. Stir occasionally.
6. Uncover and add beans.
7. Continue simmering, stirring occasionally, until beans are heated through and chili is slightly thickened, about 15 minutes. (Add water if too thick.)
8. Season to taste with salt and pepper and additional chili powder.
9. Garnish as desired.

Notes

- If you like macaroni or pasta in your chili, cook it separately and add it when you serve the chili. This will prevent the leftover pasta from becoming mushy. Freeze the chili without macaroni/pasta.
- This recipe uses about half a can of beans. Use the rest to add protein to salads or soups.
- Handy for smaller recipes: 8 oz. cartons of chicken, beef, and vegetable stock in the pantry and/or jars of concentrated soup base in the fridge.

Special Occasions

*D*ear sisters, we think about the events our beloved will miss—weddings, anniversaries, grandchildren, family reunions, holidays, family trips. They will miss these landmark events but we can experience these special days, not just for ourselves but for them as well.

How can we honor and include them in these special occasions? Here are some ideas.

- A moment of silence in their honor.
- A special prayer of gratitude for them.
- Setting out a place for them.
- A few words spoken about what this event would have meant to them.
- Words of appreciation in the event program or web site.
- Including a poem or photo they liked in the event program or on display.
- Displaying a photo of them with the graduate or bride and groom.
- Ensuring the slide show includes them.
- Setting out something they created—a fishing lure or artwork or recipe or knitted item.
- A floral arrangement with flowers or colors they loved.
- A photo set in a place of honor.
- Playing of their favorite song or music.

- Serving of their favorite dish.
- Wearing an item they gave you.
- What else?

A common worry of bereaved people is that others will move on and forget about the person we have lost. Any of the strategies above can reassure us that we are doing what we can to keep their precious memory alive.

- How might you include your beloved's memory in your upcoming events?
- Who could help you make it happen?

....

....

....

....

....

....

....

....

....

....

....

....

....

Turkey-Avocado Meatballs

Savory meatballs studded with avocado bits.

Ingredients	Directions
1 tsp. ground cumin ¼ tsp. chili powder 2 tsp. olive oil ¼ cup onion, diced 1 large clove of garlic, diced 8 oz. ground turkey 1 ripe avocado, diced ½ cup cotija, feta, or mozzarella cheese ½ tsp. freshly ground black pepper ¾ tsp. Worcestershire sauce ⅛ tsp. kosher salt (optional)	1. Preheat oven to 375°. 2. In a frying pan, toast cumin and chili. powder till fragrant, 1-2 minutes. Set aside in a medium mixing bowl. 3. Wipe out the spice pan and add olive oil. Heat oil till shimmering and add onion and garlic. Sauté for about 2-3 minutes till golden. 4. Add onion and garlic to the spices. 5. Add ground turkey, avocado, cheese Worcestershire, pepper and salt (if adding) to the bowl and mix thoroughly with a fork to combine.

6. Roll gently into
   2-ounce meatballs
   and place on baking
   sheet. (Lining the sheet
   with parchment paper
   makes cleanup so easy.)
7. Bake for 18 minutes.
   Internal temperature
   should reach 165° F.

Notes
- Serve with mashed potatoes or spinach pasta.
- These freeze beautifully.

Memorials

We are the keepers of our loved ones' stories.
They live in us and through us.

Jan Warner

*D*ear sisters, just as we can find ways to include our loved ones in special family events, we can find ways to continually keep their memory alive. People still have cemetery plots with headstones, but many people today are choosing not to have these. Here are some ideas for honoring our beloved and holding them in memory.

- Create a memory book of their life including birth certificate, photos, clippings, memorabilia.
- Create a memory quilt or pillow out of an item of their clothing.
- Purchase a special indoor plant to care for and nurture in their memory.
- Plant a memorial flower garden in their honor.
- Create a cairn, an artfully designed rock pile traditionally marking burial sites.
- Take part in a 5K run in their honor.
- Go to a place or do something that was on their bucket list.

- Write down stories about them—how you met, what they enjoyed, what challenges they conquered, etc., to share with younger family members who may have been too young to know them.
- Make a cookbook of their favorite recipes.
- Purchase a plaque on a park bench or concert hall seat or sports venue bearing their name.
- Organize an event in their name, such as a fishing or chess tournament.
- Create a web site showing their life in pictures and videos and stories.
- Create a blog to share with family and friends and invite the others to share memories.
- Establish a scholarship fund in their name.
- Fund the purchase of equipment or furniture for a church or a non-profit in their name.
- Donate to or volunteer for organizations whose mission is care or prevention of an illness they experienced.
- What else?

- Which, if any, of the ideas on the previous page for creating a memorial to your beloved might interest you?
- What different ideas for a memorial—big or small—come to your mind?
- What could be your next steps for making it happen?

Quiche Just for You

You deserve this so-very-simple French treat.

Ingredients	Directions
1 pie crust (See **Notes**) 1 large egg ¼-⅓ cup half-and-half ⅛ tsp. kosher salt 1 tsp. parsley, chopped 2 T. Parmesan cheese, grated Pinch of nutmeg 2 slices of bacon, cooked and chopped	1. Preheat oven to 425°. 2. Allow pie crust dough to warm up until it feels flexible. 3. Place dough in a small quiche dish or tart pan (about 6 inches across). Press the dough firmly around the edges, making an edging as for a pie and trimming off the extra dough. 4. Prick the bottom of the crust with a fork and bake for 12 minutes at 425° F. Remove from oven and reduce heat to 375° F. 5. Crack the egg into a measuring cup and add enough half-and-half to make a scant ½ cup.

	6. Add salt, parsley and nutmeg and mix well with a fork. 7. Scatter Parmesan and bacon pieces on the bottom of the pie crust. 8. Pour the egg mixture into crust. 9. Bake for 25 minutes. Let quiche set for at least 5 minutes.

Notes

- A pie crust from the refrigerated grocery case works better for this recipe than a frozen pie crust because it will be more flexible, easier to shape into a small quiche dish or tart pan.
- You can vary the recipe by adding several tablespoons of any cheese, sautéed mushrooms, cooked asparagus, spinach, zucchini, sausage, or any cooked seafood.

Am I Taking Care of Me?

HALT—*Hungry, Angry, Lonely, Tired?*

Author unknown

*D*ear sisters, even though we know that self-care is essential for grievers, we may find it difficult to really take care of ourselves.

Among many other impacts, grief increases inflammation in our bodies which can worsen health problems or create new ones. Grief batters our immune systems and can raise our blood pressure and the risk of blood clots. Emotional pain activates the same regions of the brain as physical pain. "If there's one thing I want people to know about grief, it's how awful it can make your body feel," writes clinical social worker Stephanie Hairston.

This journey we are on requires daily maintenance. In our misery, it can be so hard to do things for ourselves like walking outside or eating healthy meals or taking time to meditate or pray. The irony is that if we can muster the energy and focus to do these things each day for self-care, it can help us move through our pain.

This week's reflection is an opportunity to assess our current pattern of self-care. The table includes practices suggested in previous weeks or recommended by medical sources. Feel free to add your own self-care or wellness strategies.

Place an "X" in the column indicating whether you do these *daily* things Almost Always, Sometimes, or Seldom or Never.

	Things to do Every Day	Almost Always	Some-times	Sel-dom or Never
1.	I eat three meals.			
2.	I eat nutritious meals.			
3.	I drink 6-8 glasses of water.			
4.	I get outside at least once.			
5.	I move my body for 20 minutes or more.			
6.	I stop caffeine after 4 p.m.			
7.	I avoid "screen time" after 8 p.m.			
8.	I sleep at least 7 hours nightly.			
9.	I take my medications as prescribed.			
10.	I spend some time with other people.			
11.	I spend some time alone.			

	Things to do Every Day	Almost Always	Some-times	Seldom or Never
12.	I pray or meditate.			
13.	I identify what I am grateful for.			
14.	I ask for or seek out what I need.			
15.	I do something nice or comforting for myself.			
16.				
17.				

- In which areas are you taking care of yourself "Almost Aways"?
- What do you "Seldom or Never" do for self-care?
- What changes, if any, would you like to make?

Broccoli Patties

*Even children and grandchildren
will like these green veggie patties.*

Ingredients	Directions
2 cups broccoli florets ¼ cup onion, diced 1 large egg, lightly beaten ⅓ cup mozzarella or cheddar cheese, shredded ¼ tsp. garlic powder ¼ tsp. onion powder ½ tsp. kosher salt ½ tsp. black pepper ¼ cup panko crumbs Non-stick cooking spray	1. Preheat oven to 400° F. 2. Cover a small cookie sheet with parchment paper or grease sheet with nonstick cooking spray. 3. Bring a pan of water to boil and blanch broccoli for 1 minute in the water. 4. Remove and immerse broccoli in ice water to stop the cooking. 5. Dry with a clean kitchen towel or paper toweling.

6. Chop broccoli finely and mix with onion, egg, cheese, garlic powder, onion powder, salt and pepper.
7. Add panko crumbs and combine well.
8. Chill in refrigerator for 15 minutes.
9. Scoop up small portions (1-2 T.) of the mixture, shape into patties and place on prepared cookie sheet.
10. Mist patties with non-stick oil spray and bake for 10 minutes.
11. Turn the patties over and bake another 10 minutes until golden brown.

Notes
- Serve with dip from "Cauliflower Poppers" recipe.

Grief Ambush

*D*ear sisters, yesterday was a great day. It was a Wisconsin blizzard, so I didn't have to go anywhere. I tried a new pasta recipe which turned out to be delicious. I watched two episodes of a series I like and finished two crossword puzzles. I felt peaceful and happy.

Today, I am in the toilet. So sad and so heavy. It started as I heard a song on the radio. The song wasn't even over when I could feel myself sliding down into sadness. The tears fell. I miss him so painfully.

When grief ambushes, we can't think our way out of it or drink or medicate or sex or shop our way out. We can greet the grief, "Here you are," and just feel how we feel. I even asked my husband out loud if he could somehow help me get through it.

I have many days when I am warmed by memories and appreciation for the life we had together. Yet I know I will be ambushed again by grief. These painful feelings of hopelessness and loss that resurface unexpectedly do not last forever.

The painful feelings will wash over me and recede. I will let that happen as I take deep breaths and maybe get some fresh air. I trust I will feel peaceful again.

P.S. I did!

- List sounds, sights, fragrances, events that have ambushed you with grief.
- What has helped you live through these attacks?
- What else might?

Spaghetti Sauce

I share several long-kept secret ingredients here (smile).

Ingredients	Directions
2 tsp. olive oil ¼ cup onions, chopped ½ lb. ground beef 1 large garlic clove, chopped 1-14.5 oz. can diced tomatoes 1-8 oz. can tomato sauce 2 T. tomato paste ½ cup water 1-4 oz. can of mushrooms including juice ⅓ cup dry red wine ½ tsp. each of basil and oregano ¼ tsp. fennel seeds ¼ tsp. cinnamon 1 bay leaf salt and pepper to taste	1. Sauté onions and garlic lightly in olive oil (about 2 minutes) in a Dutch Oven or soup pan. 2. Add ground beef to onions until meat is browned. 3. Add remaining ingredients and stir. 4. Correct seasonings. (You might want more of the herbs.) 5. Simmer about 30 minutes, stirring occasionally. 6. Add small amount of additional water if sauce is too thick. 7. Remove bay leaf before serving. Serve on any kind of pasta.

Notes
- If you use Italian sausage instead of beef, you won't need to add fennel seeds.
- This can be made meatless as a marinara sauce and welcomes sautéed veggies at the end—zucchini, broccoli, cauliflower, really any vegetable you like.
- This sauce freezes very nicely.

Forgiveness

*D*ear sisters, who is it hardest for you to forgive:

- The friends who couldn't find time to come to the funeral?
- The family members who don't help much?
- People who said the worst, tacky things to you?
- Yourself for doing (saying) or not doing (saying) something?
- Your beloved who died, leaving you alone?

Most people harbor some ill will to someone, but it takes emotional energy to stay angry. And grieving people don't have energy to waste. So one thing we can do for ourselves is resolve to forgive other people for their thoughtlessness, unkindness, or plain meanness. Forgiving them means *disconnecting* from what they did, not accepting or condoning it.

Most importantly, forgiving them ultimately benefits us.

Forgiving others is a gift we give ourselves. Grief writer David Kessler says, "Forgiveness opens our hearts when we are stuck in the prison of resentment. We get to be right, but we never get to be happy."

Each of us is on our own path with our own world view, our own family patterns, and our own problems. And no one is perfect. Consider these options:

1. Assume that their intention was not to do harm (until proven otherwise).

2. Tell them you want to have a relationship with them (if you do), but that something they are doing or did earlier is making it hard.

3. Invite them out for coffee or lunch to reset your relationship.

4. Set boundaries with that person; have your car keys ready or an Uber account so you can leave if their behavior becomes hurtful.

5. Don't invite them to your home or accept their invitations if their behavior continues to be hurtful.

6. Shrug it off; you wouldn't want to live in that person's head.

7. Make a decision: "I don't want to carry around this ill will and therefore I forgive this person."

8. Talk with a professional therapist or grief group if you are having trouble with forgiving someone; an objective view is always helpful.

9. What else?

- Whom have you not been able to forgive?
- How would forgiving them help you now?
- What, if anything, do you want to do about it?

Salmon Cakes

*This handy recipe is a good reason to
keep a small can of salmon in your pantry.*

Ingredients	Directions
¼ cup onions, finely diced	1. In a medium bowl, combine onion, green pepper, salmon, potato flakes (or crackers or panko), egg, olive oil or butter, mayonnaise, mustard, lemon juice. and black pepper. Blend with a fork.
¼ cup green bell pepper, finely diced	
1 (6-oz.) can of salmon, drained and flaked	
⅓ cup of instant mashed potato flakes or 8 crackers, crushed (any type) or ⅓ cup panko crumbs	
1 egg, beaten	2. Form into 4 patties on a small baking sheet lined with parchment paper.
1 T. olive oil, or butter at room temperature	
2 T. mayonnaise	3. Place in the freezer for 15 minutes.
1 tsp. yellow prepared mustard	
1 T. fresh lemon juice	4. Preheat air fryer to 400°. Spray fryer basket and the patties lightly with oil.
½ tsp. ground black pepper	
Cooking oil spray (for air frying)	
Lemon wedges	

5. Air fry patties until crispy and golden, about 15 minutes. No need to flip them over. (Check them at 10 minutes.)
6. Serve with lemon wedges (or Green Velvet Cashew Sauce).

Notes

- Patties may be fried in a frying pan on medium heat. Place 3 T. olive oil in the hot pan, heat till shimmering, and carefully add the chilled patties. Fry until crispy and golden, about 6-7 minutes per side.
- I place a round screen over the frying pan to reduce splattering of hot oil.
- Leftover (cooked) fresh salmon may be used in this recipe in place of canned. Simply flake the cooked salmon and add the remaining ingredients. If mixture is too dry to stay together, add a little extra mayonnaise or olive oil.

Reaching Out

*D*ear sisters, when I started writing this book, I would tuck a few of the early word-processed pages into condolence cards. The pages assured others that a person can keep going even after the devastating loss. It helped me too. I could take the worst thing that ever happened to me and turn it into something to help others.

You know what *not* to say to someone who is grieving. You would never say things like:

- *There's a reason for everything.*
- *The good die young.*
- *You'll get over it.*
- *They're in a better place.*
- Or, the worst, *I know how you feel.*

But you would say how sorry you are and share a memory. You would ask if the bereaved person would like to talk about what happened. And you would connect after the funeral or celebration of life to offer support because you would know that people need support long after. You might invite them for a dinner together.

A lovely gift idea for a bereaved friend or family member is to put together a gift bag or box for them. I call this a "Gentle Comforts Collection." It might contain warm socks, a favorite essential oil, a journal, scented candles, chocolates, packages of dried fruit, a small glass light-catcher, fancy cookies—anything that expresses your care and concern for the specific recipient. Maybe even slip in a copy of this book.

If you feel ready, consider how to use the strength and courage you have gained over the past year to help people new to grief. Organizations exist for advocacy and finding cures for almost any disease. If you lost your beloved to illness, which one might you support or become involved with in your community? You might already be doing this and that is heroic!

If you were helped by a grief support group, you may be able to get involved as a facilitator or co-facilitator of upcoming groups to share your experience. Or perhaps you would join a group as a member simply to be there for new grievers.

We know the value of being there, witnessing grief, listening, giving a gentle hug. We can do that for others and, in the process, be comforted ourselves. We have much to offer.

- How might you use your knowledge and experiences about the process of grieving to help others?
- Are you ready to do that soon, or is it something perhaps for the future, or are you unsure? Explain.

Cauliflower Poppers

Everyone loves these poppers,
especially with the tangy dip.

Ingredients	Directions
Half of a small cauliflower (7-8 ounces) ¾ cup panko crumbs 1 garlic clove, crushed 3 T. olive oil 2 tsp. Italian seasoning 2 tsp. fresh parsley ⅓ c. finely grated Parmesan cheese 2 eggs ¼ c. flour ½ c. sour cream 3 T. plain yogurt (regular or Greek) ½ tsp. lemon juice Salt and pepper to taste Fresh chopped parsley	1. Break up cauliflower into smaller pieces (See "Notes" below). 2. Add cauliflower to lightly salted boiling water and cook for 5 minutes with lid on. Remove with slotted spoon or spider and let cool. 3. In a bowl mix panko, garlic, olive oil, Italian seasoning, parsley, Parmesan cheese. 4. Beat eggs lightly in separate bowl. 5. Dip cauliflower pieces first in flour to coat. 6. Dip pieces in egg.

7. Roll cauliflower in panko mixture till coated.
8. Place on cookie sheet lined with parchment paper.
9. Bake 15 minutes in preheated oven at 360° F.
10. For dipping sauce, combine all ingredients. Chill.

Notes
- Since these are probably going to be eaten by hand, break the cauliflower florets into big enough pieces that they can be dipped into the sauce.
- If you don't have Italian seasoning on hand, add a tsp. each of dried basil and oregano for this recipe.

Control

*D*ear sisters, we are living in the aftermath of circumstances we could not control. We could not prevent our beloved from dying. Like dominos, other parts of our life may also topple over—health, work, finances, friendships, sense of self, and more. We surely have been through something we could not control, and that awful experience can make us start to feel as if we don't have control over *anything*. (If "control" doesn't sound like the right word to you, think of it as *choices* or *agency.*)

We actually still *do* have control over many aspects of our lives. It's helpful to be reminded of them so we make good use of the power we have. Here are some things most of us still have control over. They are, in no particular order:

- With whom we spend our free time.
- With which social media we interact.
- What we commit to or decline doing for other people.
- What we commit to or decline doing for ourselves.
- What organizations we support with our time or money.
- What we think about or choose not to think about.
- What we do or don't do to move our body.
- What we do or can't do for someone else who is grieving.
- What books or podcasts or groups we seek out for support.

- How much effort (if any) we are willing to put into any given task.
- How we prepare our body and mind for sleep.
- How often we get outside in nature or stay home under our covers.
- How much time we spend worrying.
- How much we try to please other people.
- How much money we spend on non-essentials.
- How we honor and keep alive the memory of our beloved.
- How we respond (if at all) to others' words that offend or anger us.
- Whether or when we decide to find professional help in dealing with our grief.
- Whether we shop for, make, and eat nutritious or comfort food or junk foods.
- Whether we start or stop attending a faith community or change the faith community we attend.
- Whether we ask for help when we need it, and from whom we seek it.
- Which social invitations we accept, which we excuse ourselves from, and how and when we respond to them.

- Over what, if anything, on the list on the previous page do you want to take more control? Why, specifically, those?
- What things do you feel you already have control over? (Make a list of those and put it on your mirror or refrigerator.)

Egg-Lemon Soup

*This bright soup is straight
from the sunny Mediterranean.*

Ingredients	Directions
3 cups good quality low sodium chicken broth 5 T. uncooked rice (long or medium-grain) 2 eggs 1½ T. fresh lemon juice Salt to taste 1 T. fresh dill, chopped or 1 T. fresh parsley, chopped	1. In a 2-3 quart saucepan, bring chicken broth to a boil. 2. Add rice, reduce heat to low and simmer partially uncovered for about 15 minutes or until the grains are tender but not mushy. 3. Reduce heat to low. 4. Beat eggs with a whisk in a small bowl till frothy. 5. Whisk lemon juice into eggs and one or two tablespoons of the hot chicken broth (to prevent curdling). 6. Slowly add the egg-lemon mixture into the broth, stirring constantly.

	7. Cook over low heat for 2-3 minutes or until the soup thickens enough to coat a spoon. (Do not let the soup boil or it will curdle.) 8. Add salt to taste and garnish with fresh dill or parsley.

Notes

- You can add cooked, chopped chicken at the end for an even richer soup. This is a great use of a cooked rotisserie chicken.
- Add 1 tsp. of concentrated soup base if richer flavor is needed.

A New Path

*T*roubling, persistent memories or thoughts can be compared to paths through the woods. The more we walk along a path, the bigger and deeper it becomes and it will become our preferred path—easy to see and familiar. We will default to it unconsciously. This happens as readily in our brains as it does in the woods.

Unfortunately, the path of persistent thoughts tends to be of negative experiences or situations we regret.

When I first lost Matt, I was tormented by events the night of his death. I kept reliving that horrible night and beating myself up for falling asleep with my head on his bed in his last hours. Never mind that I had been awake for 48 hours in the hospital by then—the scene played and replayed in my mind. Why couldn't I stay awake?

I knew that reliving these painful thoughts was not good for me, but I didn't know how to stop it. My therapist suggested I create three affirmations or positive statements that I would write down and say to myself every morning or whenever I started going down the painful path in my mind.

The idea was to create a new path for my brain to follow. She said it didn't even matter if I believed in affirmations or even believed in these affirmations.

So my three affirmations I wrote and repeated out loud every morning were these:

- I am calm and centered.
- I live in the present.
- I see my life unfolding perfectly.

When I would find myself overcome with obsessive thoughts about that night, I would repeat my affirmations. I don't understand how it all works, but repeating these affirmations did help me replace the nightmarish thoughts I had been defaulting to.

P.S. I recently found myself obsessing over another issue. I again turned to my three affirmations, saying them out loud every time I felt myself going down that path. As I write this postscript, I don't even remember what the issue was! Voilà!

- List three affirmations you can say every day in order to create a preferred path for your mind to follow. (Feel free to use any of the ones on the previous page.)

Shrimp Alfredo

*For a special occasion—
shrimp enrobed in a creamy sauce*

Ingredients	Directions
4 oz. fettuccine, uncooked ¼ cup pasta cooking water 8 oz. peeled and deveined medium shrimp, uncooked 1 green onion, white and green parts, chopped 1 garlic clove, minced 1 T. olive oil ⅓ cup fresh Parmesan cheese, grated 3 T. half-and-half or cream 2 T. cream cheese ⅛ tsp. ground black pepper 1 T. fresh parsley, chopped	1. Cook pasta in salted water according to package directions but with no oil. 2. Drain pasta, reserving ¼ c. cooking water. 3. Combine shrimp, onion, and garlic in a bowl. 4. Heat a skillet over medium heat. Add oil and swirl to coat. 5. Sauté shrimp mixture 4 minutes or until shrimp are done, stirring occasionally. 6. Remove shrimp from pan and set aside. 7. Reduce heat and add pasta cooking water to skillet.

8. Add Parmesan, half-and-half or cream, cream cheese, and black pepper to skillet. Cook, stirring constantly with a wire whisk for 2 minutes or until Parmesan cheese melts.
9. Add shrimp and pasta and gently combine.
10. Sprinkle with parsley.

Notes:
- To end up with 8 oz. of shelled shrimp, you will need a 12 oz. package of unshelled shrimp.
- Refrigerated fresh fettuccine is very nice with this recipe, but not essential.
- Shrimp are cooked when they are no longer gray and translucent. When cooked through, they will be white with pink or red markings.

My Own True North

Dear sisters, the word "bereave" is derived from several different and very old languages—Middle English, Germanic, Saxon, Dutch, and others. Meanings include breaking, tearing apart, taking away by violence, robbing, seizing. That is surely how it feels.

We are torn apart. We realize we will never be the same person we were. This is inevitable. How could we be when such a huge part of ourselves is gone?

So we ask ourselves, "If I'm not who I was, then who am I?" A great question to ask. Finding and rebuilding ourselves and who we are after our loss is what allows us to ultimately say "Yes" to life. Grief writer David Kessler says:

> We have to say goodbye to the life we had and say yes to the future. He will always be a part of me, and one of my goals is to figure out who I am in this future without him. That is how I will begin to rebuild.

How do we rebuild ourselves? I believe it starts with identifying our own values—what are our bedrock beliefs and attitudes that underlie everything we think, say, and do?

Examples of common values are things like honesty, clear communication, kindness, spirituality, family, equity, loyalty, self-control, tradition, work ethic, affection, environment, financial success, frugality, and the like. Life goes so much more smoothly if we can live according to our values. Conversely, if our life is out of sync with our values, we cannot be happy, at least for long.

Many bereaved people question the values they once held. Our lives have been disassembled by death. A surviving partner may wonder if her values are really her values or whether they came along with the relationship, no matter how loving.

The questions on the next page provide an opportunity to highlight our own "true north"—the values most important to us. These values can be the building blocks of "a new normal" for us.

- List ten of your most important values and beliefs. Check those you shared with your loved one.
- Circle the top three values and beliefs you want to be "true north" as you recreate your "new normal."

Citrus Salad

*Especially wonderful when oranges
and grapefruits are in peak season.*

Ingredients	Directions

¼ cup orange juice
1 T. finely chopped shallot
  or sweet onion
1 T. pure maple syrup
1 T. Dijon mustard
¼ tsp. kosher salt
¼ tsp. black pepper
6 T. extra virgin olive oil
 	
1 orange
1 tangerine
½ small red grapefruit
2 cups of romaine lettuce,
  torn into bite-sized
  pieces
¼ cup fresh parsley,
  chopped
	1. Combine orange juice and shallot in a bowl; set aside and let it rest for 5 minutes.
	2. Whisk in maple syrup, mustard, salt, and pepper. Gradually whisk in oil until well-blended and set aside.
	3. Cut away the peel and the white pith of the citrus fruits and slice into ¼ inch thick rounds.
	4. To make one salad, layer half of the romaine and half of the citrus rounds on a plate.

| ¼ cup roasted almonds, chopped ¼ cup Manchego or Parmesan cheese, shaved | 5. Top with half the parsley and half the almonds and cheese. Drizzle with dressing. |

Notes
- This makes two big salads and extra dressing. Add the dressing to the second salad just before you are ready to eat it.

Living in the Present

Yesterday's the past,
tomorrow's the future,
but today is a gift.
That's why it's called the present.

Bil Keane

*D*ear sisters, in the coming months and years, we don't have to choose between grieving for our beloved and living our own lives fully. We can love and commemorate our life companion and also have a peaceful, satisfying, even happy, life. One way to find this "both-and" balance is by living in the present.

Admittedly living in the present is a tall order for us when all we want to do is turn the clock back to when we had our beloved living with us in the world. Yet living in the present can help us deal with our grief and pain.

Even when our loved one was still living, how often did we barrel through our days thinking about the past or the future—worrying, regretting, ruminating—barely noticing what we were doing? It's a common pattern in modern life.

Living in the present means we feel the painful feelings as they come, not trying to avoid or quash them. We know that a feeling will eventually move along, especially if we are willing to sit with it, acknowledge it. And we don't judge our feelings or our reactions. We accept them with compassion as they are.

Living in the present means we pay attention to what is happening right now in this moment. If we are washing our hands, we are appreciating the warm water and suds. If we are walking, we pay attention to the flowers that just came out or the beautiful sunset. If we are with children or grandchildren, we are present to them, listening with ears and heart. If we are sitting down to a meal, we pause to enjoy and appreciate what is in front of us.

Eckhart Tolle says, "The present moment is all you ever have. There is never a time when your life is not 'this moment.'" To help stay in the present moment, he advises that we do one thing at a time and focus on that one thing. (*Adios* multi-tasking.) "Focus not on the 100 things that you will or may have to do at some future time but on the one thing that you can do now."

Another tool for staying in the present is the breathing exercise in this book ("Hard to Breathe"), which can help you stay grounded. Yoga, Qi-Gong, and meditation are helpful options too.

If our faith carries with it the promise of life after death, what better way to honor the time we have been given on Earth than to live it with full awareness and appreciation?

- How often do you find yourself thinking of the past or the future without paying attention to the present?
- Describe times when you and your beloved were together, truly living in the present, without thinking of past or future.
- What helps you stay aware of the present moment now?

Red Beans and Rice

I make this for every Mardi Gras,
but you can enjoy it anytime.

Ingredients	Directions
2 tsp. olive oil ¼ cup onion, diced ¼ cup green bell pepper, diced ½ cup celery, diced 1 clove garlic, minced ½ cup dry kidney beans 2 cups good quality beef broth ¼ tsp. thyme ¼ tsp. oregano ½ bay leaf ½ tsp. smoked paprika Pinch of fresh ground black pepper Pinch of cayenne pepper Cooked white or brown rice	1. Check over and rinse dry beans. Place in a bowl and add cold water to cover beans by two inches. Refrigerate overnight. 2. Finely dice the onion, green pepper, and celery and mince the garlic. 3. Heat oil in a heavy-bottom pot over medium heat. Sauté vegetables till softened (3-5 minutes). 4. Rinse and drain soaked beans in a colander and add them to the pot.

5. Add broth, thyme, oregano, bay leaf, smoked paprika, and a pinch each of freshly ground pepper and cayenne pepper. Stir.

6. Cover pot and bring to full boil over high heat. When it reaches a boil, turn heat down to low and simmer for two hours.

7. Check to be sure it is simmering. Increase heat if necessary. Stir occasionally, add more broth or water if sticking. Keep lid on.

8. After two hours (or longer), the beans should be soft and tender. Mash some of the beans in the pot to thicken things up.

9. Remove the lid and bay leaf. Simmer for another 30 minutes more to help it thicken.

Notes
- Serve over brown or white rice.
- Kidney beans must be fully cooked. Undercooked kidney beans can cause illness.
- Create a vegan dish by using vegetable broth in place of beef broth.

Progress

I assure you, the one you lost will always be with you.
Always be with you.
The day will come when their memory
brings a smile to your lips
before it brings a tear to your eye,
as unbelievable as that is now.
It will take a while.

Joseph R. Biden

*D*ear sisters, we are surviving the most stressful thing that can happen, the death of our partner in life. Our own future is still to be written. The next challenge is not merely to survive, as it was at first. Each year after our loss can bring its own challenges, but our task is to find meaning in our lives and reconfigure how we want to live now. Grief writer David Kessler says:

> Ultimately meaning comes through finding a way to sustain your love for the person after their death while you are moving forward with your life. That doesn't mean you'll stop missing [them] but it does mean that you will experience a heightened awareness of how precious life is.

We all have within ourselves the potential and ability to do amazing things despite our pain and sometimes even because of it. The strategies suggested here will serve us well in the coming months and years, and we will probably find new and creative ways to use them.

The longing for our beloved life companion does not disappear, no matter how much time has passed, but we can figure out how to take the love with us as we go forward into the future. Hopefully we can all imagine more healing and life-affirming growth to come in the years ahead.

- Write a letter to the beloved partner you have lost, relating your grief journey and sharing your hopes. What have you learned? What changes have you made in yourself? How have you grown? What has been most difficult for you?
- What questions do you still have?

....

....

....

....

....

....

....

....

....

....

....

Weeknight Clam Linguini

Seriously satisfying seafood flavor,
without any clam shells to scrub!

Ingredients	Directions
2 tsp. olive oil 4 green onions, sliced (white and tender green parts) 1 garlic clove, minced ⅛ to ¼ tsp. red pepper flakes (to taste) 1-6½ oz. can of clams, chopped and drained (save liquid) ¼ cup dry white wine 1 T. fresh basil, chopped or 1 tsp. dried basil ½ tsp. dried oregano 4 oz. uncooked linguini (or 2 cups hot, cooked linguini) 1 T. Parmesan cheese, grated ½ cup of pasta cooking water reserved	1. Cook linguini according to package directions. Save out ½ cup of cooking water. Drain and return pasta to pan to keep warm. 2. Heat olive oil in medium skillet till glistening (but not smoking). 3. Add green onions, garlic and pepper flakes. Sauté till softened, 1-3 minutes. 4. Add the clams and sauté briefly (about 1 minute) to blend the flavors. 5. Add clam liquid, wine, basil, and oregano and bring to a gentle boil.

6. Reduce heat and simmer, covered, 8-9 minutes till slightly thickened.
7. Add cooked linguini to the sauce and toss to coat. (Add pasta water by tablespoons if sauce has become too thick.)
8. Sprinkle with Parmesan cheese and serve.

Notes
- Remember to share your favorite recipes with others who might be grieving.

References

Ashworth, D. (2022). *Loss: Poems to Better Weather the Many Waves of Grief.* Black & White Publishing.

Aurelius, Marcus (171-175 CE). *The Meditations.*

Bernstein, E. (May 31, 2020). "Feeling Upset? Try This Special Writing Technique," *Wall Street Journal.* https://www.wsj.com/articles/feeling-upset-try-this-special-writing-technique-/.

Biden, J. (2021). *Joe Biden & Kamala Harris Speech on Violence Against AAPI Community at Emory Transcript.* https://www.whitehouse.gov/briefing-room/speeches-remarks/2021/03/19/remarks-by-president-biden-at-emory-university/.

Didion, J. (2005). *A Year of Magical Thinking.* Vintage.

Harvard Medical School (Feb. 2, 2021). "Exercise is an all-natural treatment to fight depression." https://www.health.harvard.edu/mind-and-mood/.

Fagundes, P., *et al.* (August 2021)."Biological mechanisms underlying widowhood's health and consequences: Does diet play a role?" *Comprehensive Psychoneuroendocrinology* . Vol 7. https://www.sciencedirect.com/science/.

Hairston, S. (2019). *How Grief Shows Up in Your Body.* https://www.webmd.com/special-reports/.

Haley, E. (2015). *Feeling Nothing During Grief: The Experience of Emotional Numbness.* https://whatsyourgrief.com/feeling-nothing-during-grief/.

Haley, E. (2017). *Grief Is Like.* https://whatsyourgrief.com/grief-is-like/.

Haley, E. (2022). *64 Reminders if You're Filled with Holiday Dread.* https://whatsyourgrief.com/holiday-dread/.

Haley, E. & Williams, L. (2022). *What's Your Grief: Lists to Help You Through Any Loss*. Quirk Books.

Harrold, J. (2023). *Why Rituals Matter (and How to Create Your Own)*. https://www.mindful.org/.

Hanson, R. (2021). *Do Positive Experiences Stick to Your Ribs?* https://www.rickhanson.net/.

Kessler, D. (2019). *Finding Meaning: The Sixth Stage of Grief*. Scribner.

Kodanaz, R. (2013). *Living with Loss, One Day at a Time*. Fulcrum Publishing.

Lambin, H. (1998). *The Death of a Husband: Reflections for a Grieving Wife*. ACTA.

Noel, B. & Blair, P. (2008). *I Wasn't Read to Say Goodbye: Surviving, Coping & Healing after the Sudden Death of a Loved One*. Sourcebooks.

Puddicombe, A. (2021). *Falling in Love with Life*. [video] Headspace.

Shaw, L. (2017). *Your Brain is Boss*. SRA Books.

Stroebe, M., Stroebe, W. & Abakoumkin, G. (Nov. 2005). "The Broken Heart: Suicide Ideation in Bereavement." *American Journal of Psychiatry.* 162(11):2178-80. https://pubmed.ncbi.nlm.nih.gov/16263862/.

Tolle, E. (1999). *The Power of Now*. New World Library.

University of Rochester Health Center. (2023). *Journaling and Mental Health.* https://www.urmc.rochester.edu/encyclopedia/content/.

Warner, J. (2018). *Grief Day by Day: Simple Practices and Daily Guidance for Living with Loss*. Althea Press.

Recipe Index

About the Author

Photo by Ann Zanzig

*K*athleen A. Paris, Ph.D., shares her own grief journey here following the death in 2018 of her husband, Matt Cullen.

As an author and management consultant, Paris has assisted organizations over the past thirty years to plan for new realities and improve their systems and organizational climate. She currently holds the title of Distinguished Consultant Emeritus from the University of Wisconsin-Madison.

Paris has consulted in the United States and internationally in Canada, Cyprus, France, Guam, Switzerland, Virgin Islands, and the UK. She is an editor and one of the co-authors of *Bending Granite: 30+ True Stories of Leading Change (ACTA, 2022)*.

Among many other books and articles, Paris has written *Staying Healthy in Sick Organizations: The Clover Practice*™ and *Bringing Your Strategic Plan to Life*.

She lives in Madison, Wisconsin, and shares with her late husband their five treasured children and thirteen grandchildren.

Acknowledgments

Sincerest thanks to friends and family who helped test the recipes here—Elizabeth Fadell, Mary Ellen O'Grady, Patty and Don McKinnon, Sandy and Bruce Salvo, and Ann Zanzig. Karen Redfield, Lynn Thomas, and Marian Timmerman were invaluable in editing and proofing the manuscript. Thanks also to Miri Zena McDonald and Marti Sopher for assistance with communications.

I am thankful, also, to Gregory Pierce, ACTA Publications' editor and publisher, for recognizing immediately the need for this book and its potential for bringing comfort to grieving women (and maybe even to some grieving men).

Books on Loss and Grief

An A-Z Guide to Letting Go; Constructing a New Normal; and *Prayers for Difficult Times* by Helen Reichert Lambin

Born to Fly: An Infant's Journey to God by Cindy Claussen

Catholic and Mourning a Loss: 5 Challenges and 5 Opportunities for Catholics to Live and Mourn through a Loss by Mauryeen O'Brien

An Empty Space in Your Heart: Reflections on the Death of a Sibling or Best Friend by Helen Reichert Lambin; *Death of a Child* by Elaine Stillwell; *Death of a Husband* by Helen Reichert Lambin, *Death of a Parent* by Delle Chapman; and *Death of a Wife* by Robert Vogt

First Tears after the Loss of Your Child by Linda Anderson

A Gathering of Angels: Seeking Healing after an Infant's Death by Victoria Leland, Linda Bailey, and Audra Fox-Murphy

God Shed His Grace on Thee: Moving Remembrances of 50 American Catholics compiled by Carol DeChant

Grieving with Mary by Mary K. Doyle

How We Can Suffer Our Sorrow: And Become Wiser, Better, Gentler People by Pamela Smith

Sorrow Like No Other: Supporting the Grief of Parents Whose Child Has Died by Charley and Diane Monaghan

**Available from booksellers or
www.actapublications.com 800-397-2282**